HOOSIER AUTUMN

The Remarkable Story of
Indiana University's
1945 Championship Football Team

ROBERT D. ARNOLD

Foreword by Indiana University's
Basketball Coach Bob Knight
with Bob Hammel

Guild Press of Indiana, Inc.
Indianapolis

GUILD PRESS OF INDIANA
6000 Sunset Lane
Indianapolis, IN 46208

Library of Congress
Catalog Card Number
96-76829

Hardcover ISBN 1-878208-86-1
Paperback ISBN 1-878208-85-3

Manufactured in the United States of America

This book is dedicated to the players and coaches of Indiana's 1945 football team and to the memory of those deceased.

You made those Saturday afternoons in the fall of 1945 something special that I'll remember all my life.

You were my heroes then. You still are.

CONTENTS

ACKNOWLEDGMENTS

The remembrances contained in this book could not have been assembled without the cooperation and support of the living members of the 1945 Indiana team. The university alumni office was kind enough to supply me with addresses and some phone numbers of the players who had maintained contact with the university. Unfortunately, despite repeated attempts, I was unable to reach some members. End Lou Mihajlovich died during the latter stages of my interviewing and, out of respect to his family, I opted not to call, though he was an integral part of the team.

Twenty-two players were interviewed, along with three very special ladies—Dixie Brown, Barbara Goldsberry, and Eleanor Kluszewski, who shared with me their memories of Howard, John, and Ted, along with other members of the team. Only one player declined to be interviewed, which was his prerogative. He said he was too young then. Weren't we all?

Special thanks go to the following former players though some of them are mentioned rarely in the narrative. Their recollections and their generosity in sharing them are much appreciated: Charlie Armstrong—tackle at 175 pounds, backed up Goldsberry in addition to kicking duties, in Florida State Athletic Hall of Fame; Bill Bradley—halfback, also ran track for Indiana, professor of physical education at Western Illinois University; Wally Getz—end, spent thirty-eight years with GE; Bob Harbison—guard, spent career coaching football at Florida State, Florida State Athletic Hall of Fame; Bob Joseph—tackle, retired after forty-one years as teacher, coach, and principal at Gary's Calumet High School; Bob Meyer—center, teacher and coach at Arsenal Technical High School in Indianapolis, until retiring in 1986; Bob Miller—tailback, backed-up two All-Americans in Hoernsmeyer and Taliaferro, played baseball at IU; Larry Napolitan—end, retired in 1992 as vice-president and general manager of a manufacturing concern; John Roper—tackle, at 6 feet 5 inches, also played basketball at IU, lives in Hammond,

Indiana; Nick Sebek—quarterback, IU's most valuable player in 1949, played professionally with Washington Redskins; Tom Schwartz—end, Indiana Mr. Basketball of 1945, left football for basketball in 1946, retired executive vice-president of Lomas Corporation, lives with wife Pat in Naples, Florida; and Howard Wright—tackle, first alternate to West Point before coming to Indiana, retired and living in Vincennes, Indiana.

In Indianapolis, thanks go to Gordon Smith, Bob Riddell, and Jim Haramy for their support and encouragement. To sports announcer Tom Carnegie, who shared his many memories on a hot summer afternoon in Zionsville. To my congenial and expert typist, Margaret Elsea. To my editor, Dave Powell, who in addition to possessing all the requisite professional skills, also happens to be a nice guy. And last but not least, to my wife, Linda, for support and interest in this project.

In Bloomington, thanks to the university archives staff for their interest, photographs and tolerance of my frequent visits to review 1945 issues of the *Indiana Daily Student*. To my sounding board of long standing, Thomas Lincoln Plimpton, whose continued championing of the book at our Monday lunches at Nick's kept me going. Thanks also to Bob Hammel, former sports editor of the *Bloomington Herald-Times,* for his insight and contact with Coach Bob Knight. And where would I have been without the wisdom of eighty-two-year-young Bob Cook, IU class of 1935, an assistant athletic director under Bo McMillin and an inveterate booster of Indiana University sports? He not only provided me with his extensive collection of photographs, he also permitted me to use excerpts from his 1994 biography of McMillin (available through the university's Varsity Club).

Finally, to Indiana University Chancellor Herman B Wells, for the hour we spent together last summer at his home on Tenth Street. I left with his heartening words: "Good luck on your book, young man. Save me a copy."

That was all the encouragement I needed.

Indiana University Archives

The end of the war marked the beginning of excellence for Indiana's 1945 football squad. Nine World War II returnees, including stars Howard Brown and Pete Pihos, helped the Hoosiers post their unforgettable championship season. From left, kneeling: Brown, Pihos and Russ Deal. From left, standing: Leroy Stovall, Allan Horn, Frank Ciolli, Bill Buckner, Charlie Armstrong, and John Kokos.

FOREWORD

I was a history major in college, but I can't honestly say my interest in historic events started early enough for me to have my own memories of the 1945 football season at Indiana University.

I turned five when they were about halfway through that season. Even if my memories had started accumulating that early, I doubt that in Orrville, Ohio, they were giving the kind of attention to that Indiana football team that it truly deserved.

Since coming to Indiana, though, I feel I have achieved a familiarity with that team and its accomplishments. More than that, I have built a deep respect and an admiration for the effort, the determination, the dedication that that unusual group of men was able to put into that 9–0–1 season.

My link with it came from meeting and getting to know and to like many of the players who were so vital to the team's success. I would present five players as examples—Howard Brown, Pete Pihos, Bob Ravensberg, George Taliaferro, and Ted Kluszewski.

Ted is gone now, but no team, no university could have had a better lifetime representative than big, friendly, sincere, conscientious Ted Kluszewski. I got to know him as the batting coach for the Cincinnati Reds. I knew of him, of course, from his own playing days. Not many people realize that Ted, who epitomized raw power with those bulging arms coming out from the sleeveless jerseys the Reds wore in his playing days, ranked with Lou Gehrig and Joe DiMaggio and probably fewer than a handful of others in baseball history in a truly special achievement: more home runs than strikeouts while hitting forty or more homers in a season.

Ted did it three times in a row: 40 homers and 34 strikeouts in 1953; 49 homers (his career high) and 35 strikeouts in 1954; and 47 homers and 40 strikeouts in 1955. He led the major leagues in both home runs and RBI (141) in that 1954 season, when he hit .326. He hit over .300 seven times and averaged .298 for his fifteen-year career. Of today's players, the only one to come close to those homer-to-strikeout numbers is another of my personal favorites, Don Mattingly (35 homers, 41 strikeouts in 1985). That's the kind of hitter, competitor and athlete you talk about when the subject is Ted Kluszewski. And that is why the best players on the best baseball team I ever was around—Johnny Bench, Joe Morgan, Pete Rose, Tony Perez and the others of the "Big Red Machine" of the 1970s—listened to Ted and loved the guy. He didn't have an easy job as batting coach of that team, but he did it very well because he had the respect of even those great players.

It also was obvious to me that he was proud of his Indiana University ties and of the key contributions he made as a sophomore to that 1945 football team. His love for Indiana carried over into our basketball program. I always knew we had him as a fan.

It was basketball that introduced me to all of the others I mentioned, except maybe Pete Pihos. As a boy, I picked out some of the greatest players in all of the major league sports and wrote to some, requesting autographed pictures. One who responded was the great Philadelphia Eagles end, Pete Pihos. Years later, I was at Indiana and I met him. In the late summer of 1981, after we had all been staggered by the auto accident injuries that paralyzed Landon Turner, I was in Fort Wayne at a fund-raising dinner for Landon. Pete had a major role in that event, and we sat together, sharing some conversation. When I spoke, I mentioned getting that signed picture back from him, and that he had signed it: "Lots of luck, Pete Pihos." I've heard since then that Pete has told people he thought I was just spreading some malarkey to make him sound good till I mentioned that phrase. "I knew then that he was telling the truth," he told a friend of mine. "That's the way I always signed them."

George Taliaferro was one of the first people I met after taking the job in Bloomington. Right from the start, and for many, many years after that, he was a big help for us in recruiting. He played a big role in helping us get our program started.

Bob Ravensberg—"Raven"—is not someone I have spent a lot of time with, but I have really enjoyed the occasions when he did get to Bloomington for a game or an event or when our paths crossed in St. Louis or elsewhere.

I've saved for last a very, very special friend and person. No one was better to me or more helpful to me in those early years in Bloomington than Howard Brown. His love for Indiana University was legendary, and not one of the legends overstated it. When we had some tough losses, Howard was always right there, and the really good times were a little better because I knew how much Howard was enjoying them. The university lost a great representative when Howard died April 4, 1975, and Indiana basketball—and the Indiana basketball coach—lost a dear friend.

I never met Bo McMillin. I can only conclude from the caliber of people he brought in to play for him, the ones I have been lucky enough over the years to get to know, that he was more than just the obviously great football coach that his record shows him to be. He knew that great teams don't happen without great people. That's what this book is all about.

— Indiana University basketball coach Bob Knight (with Bob Hammel), April 1996

INTRODUCTION

The referee's gun went off at 3:45 P.M. that Saturday, November 24, 1945, signaling the end of one of the great sport stories of the decade. For the first time since its admission to the Big Ten Conference in 1899, Indiana University had finally won a football championship. A 26–0 victory that afternoon over traditional rival Purdue had earned this Hoosier team its place in history.

As the sun cast long shadows onto the field at Bloomington, hundreds of fans in the overflow crowd streamed onto the turf to congratulate the players and coach Bo McMillin. The celebration would continue well into the night, and few of the twenty-seven thousand fans who stretched tiny Memorial Stadium well beyond its capacity would forget that chilly autumn afternoon.

Thanks to World War II, this Indiana team had taken five years to build. And it was a diverse group—a mix of battle-hardened war veterans and wet-behind-the-ears freshmen, of rural whites and big-city blacks. Indeed, this team was a puzzle whose pieces seemed at first glance not to fit: a baseball slugger who didn't like to practice, a junior tackle with a bum leg, a hard-throwing quarterback too short to see over his linemen, a one-eyed tackle, a fire-breathing fullback with an ego to match. Yet somehow, guided by a coach who combined innovation, paternalism and eccentricity in just the right measure, this unlikely group became something bigger than its disparate parts. It became a team—one that earned collective honor and individual success.

Nine of the eleven Indiana players who started in that Purdue game later played professional football and one played professional baseball. But it was on this November day in 1945, with the world rising from the ashes of a devastating war, that these young men preserved their place in the American memory. They were Big Ten football champs—the first ones, and still the only undefeated team in Indiana University history. This, then, is a story of champions—of McMillin's "po' little boys" and the special season they shared with a newly hopeful nation.

—1—
STARTING OVER

In the rain and cold of a January afternoon, a lone student hurried across the Indiana University campus in Bloomington, anxious to escape the weather that had welcomed in the new year of 1945. Near-zero temperatures and snow were predicted that night. The next day, Indiana University would welcome another class of incoming students—only three hundred, but the university had become accustomed to smaller wartime enrollments. In fact, colleges and universities across the county for the past four years had learned to cope with shortages of coal, food, rubber—and students. Throughout the state of Indiana, only 18,096 college students were enrolled.

As the early-winter darkness enveloped the campus, students huddled inside, gathering around their radios to hear the broadcast of the New Year's Day football game from Pasadena, California. Tennessee and Southern California were playing for the Rose Bowl title. The students can be forgiven if they voiced the hope that someday their Hoosiers would play on New Year's Day. After all, it was a time for hope in America, hope that had been bought—and was still being paid for—by soldiers' blood half a world away.

That January, after years of distant death and domestic deprivation, the war news took a positive turn. In fact, the successes seem to come hard on each other's heels:

- The Allies had invaded Luzon in the Philippines to start the year, while bombs rained on Berlin and the Germans' last-gasp effort at the Battle of the Bulge faltered.
- In February, Stalin, Churchill, and the newly inaugurated Roosevelt met at Yalta to carve up the postwar world.
- The Nazis surrendered on May 7, allowing U.S. forces to concentrate on their methodical march toward the main island of Japan. It was a march that cost tens of thousands of Ameri-

1

can lives before early August, when two atomic blasts brought it—and the war—to an abrupt end.

Against this larger-than-life backdrop, the small routines of campus life went on, with some wartime alterations, of course. The movies provided some escape, particularly the Harris Grand Theatre where, in late March, only those eighteen years of age or older were permitted to view *Escort Girl* "(Sure I have a sister, mister.") A hot bowl of chili at Rolls' Grill concluded the evening (only twenty-five cents). And even though the junior prom dinner was canceled for "lack of interest," the formal season closed on a high note with the actual junior prom dance the evening of March 24. Finally, two days after President Roosevelt's death, the seniors bade IU farewell with a dinner and dance on Saturday, April 14, and graduation the next day. The baseball and track seasons continued on into early June, but many fans had already set their sights on another sport—summer football practice.

On June 25, 1945, a group of muscular young men lined up in Indiana's steaming fieldhouse to receive their gear. These athletes, Indiana's freshman football class for the fall, all were anxious to earn a place on the varsity squad before classes began in late September. Standing out among them was 6-foot-5, 210-pound Tom Schwartz of Kokomo, not only a great football prospect, but also Indiana's "Mr. Basketball" for 1945. Also impressive was 235-pound lineman John Goldsberry from South Bend, an All-State player who was sure to contribute in 1945. Next to Goldsberry and Schwartz was George Taliaferro, a running back from Gary Roosevelt High School who, at 5 feet 11 inches and 185 pounds, combined power and quickness. These freshmen would have until July, when the varsity players were to return, to make a good impression. And the man they needed to impress was twelfth-year head coach Alvin Nugent McMillin, better known to the public and his players as "Bo."

McMillin, a fifty-year-old, Texas-born charmer whose gray hair and lined face lent him a grandfatherly air, had long ago tagged the Hoosiers his "po' little boys." For years, Bo had fought an uphill battle for respect in the Big Ten, then also known as the Western Conference. As a football doormat, the Hoosiers had never received more than marginal consideration when conference games were scheduled. The powers—Michigan, Minnesota, Illinois, Ohio State—simply refused to play Indiana regularly;

and when they did play, the games were seldom scheduled for Bloomington. (Who could blame them? Seventy-five thousand fans at Ann Arbor or Columbus versus perhaps twenty thousand at Bloomington meant fatter paydays for both teams.) In fact, the Hoosiers' schedule was so heavily tilted toward away games that McMillin's 17–11–4 record for his first four years at Indiana was a minor miracle. Of these thirty-two games from 1934 through 1937, only twelve were played at home.

For 1945, despite excellent recruiting that had led to fine seasons the previous two years—including a seven-win campaign in 1944, McMillin and athletic director Zora Clevenger reluctantly accepted Indiana's continuing role as a conference outsider. They announced a home slate that included Nebraska, Tulsa, the Bunker Hill Naval Station (later replaced by Cornell College of Iowa), and annual rival Purdue. On the road the Hoosiers would face Illinois, Northwestern, Iowa, Pittsburgh, Minnesota, and mighty Michigan, which had lowered itself to play host to the Hoosiers to open the season.

On July 3, rejecting offers from the newly formed All American Football Conference, Bo agreed to a new ten-year contract with Indiana at $9,500 per year. He would also be a professor of physical education. A week later, Professor McMillin's freshman squad had grown to forty-eight as he and his coaches prepared for that fall's ten-game schedule. Bo had never had a surplus of assistant coaches and, after losing two to the service, he got by with John Kovatch and Paul "Pooch" Harrell, augmented by Indiana wrestling coach Charlie McDaniel and track and field coach Gordon Fisher. Lettermen returning for 1945 included Al Horn, John Cannady, Bob Miller, Bill Armstrong, Bob Meyer, Chet Sanders, Ben Raimondi, Bob Ravensberg, Frank Ciolli, Dick Deranek, Joe Sowinski, Ted Kluszewski, and Lou Mihajlovich. Besides Schwartz, Goldsberry, and Taliaferro, other notable freshmen included sprinter Bill Bradley from Rushville, state high school scoring leader Jackie Adams from Muncie, Pat Kane from Marion, and quarterback Nick Sebek.

In early August, cheered by Japan's surrender, Indiana continued its daily practice routine, heartened by the news that three veterans were set to return to campus. Lineman John Kokos, who had flown thirty-five B-17 missions over Europe, was on his way. Letterman Russ "Mutt" Deal had called Bo and said, "I'll be back September first." And halfback Jimmy Dewar was in Chicago for the College All-Star game and had hinted at his return.

On August 18 summer drills ended. An intrasquad game high-lighted Indiana's offensive power as quarterback Ben Raimondi led his red squad over the black team 36–6. Versatile John Cannady stood out at fullback. "Good team spirit and overall willingness to work hard are the chief rays of sunshine," said Bo. He mourned the loss of 1944 stars John Tavener and Harry "Chick" Jagade and felt the freshmen would be called on early to relieve some trouble areas. "Speed is lacking," he said, "but we're big enough." With the draft still in effect, he feared he'd lose some of his freshmen, so he hoped for the return of more veterans.

But Bo spent far more time working than he did hoping, and one of the things he and the Hoosiers experimented with in practice was the new T-formation. Although the deceptive single-wing formation still had its devotees—McMillin included—major schools were finding the T to their liking. In the T-formation, the quarterback lined up directly behind the center while the other three backs lined up side by side several yards behind the quarterback. The quarterback took the ball from center, and the play began. Bo, ever the innovator, had devised what he referred to as a "cockeyed T," using an unbalanced line with one of the backs set out near the end. The quarterback had the option of either taking the center snap or stepping back and to the side so the snap would go directly to the tailback for a single-wing play. On the defensive side, McMillin had his ends step back from the line of scrimmage just before the snap, leaving only four down line-men. As a result, two of the opposing linemen were left with no one to block.

As the Hoosiers' date with Michigan approached, Bo prepared his starting lineup. At end: Ted Kluszewski, a 1944 starter at 6 feet 2 inches, 205 pounds, and Bob Ravensberg, a superb defender and pass receiver. At tackle: ex-serviceman Russ "Mutt" Deal and big freshman John Goldsberry. At guard: lettermen Frank Ciolli and Joe Sowinski. And at center: Bob Meyer, a 5-foot 10-inch, 195-pound sophomore from Indianapolis' Arsenal Technical High School.

Starting at quarterback: 1944 reserve Ben Raimondi, a fine passer who had shone in practice despite an early shoulder injury. A 1945 rule change would make Raimondi's passing even more effective. Unlike previous years, when the passer could only drop back so many yards from the line of scrimmage, passes this season could be thrown from anywhere behind the line. In the backfield, McMillin penciled in freshman George Taliaferro from Gary and Dick Deranek, a returning star from the 1944 squad. At fullback, Bo started 175-pound freshman Nick Lysohir.

Reserves sure to see action at Michigan were sophomore Mel Groomes, a lightning-quick halfback, and Lou Mihajlovich, a second-year end from South Bend. But overall Indiana wasn't deep. Many of the starters were expected to play sixty minutes at Ann Arbor.

Conversely, Michigan, which had come within a few minutes of winning the 1944 conference championship, returned ten lettermen along with several Navy and Marine trainees. Supplementing this group was a typical Wolverine cast of outstanding freshmen. And just to twist Bo's tail a bit, word out of Ann Arbor on game week said Michigan's 1944 star halfback, Bob Nussenbaum, was out of the service and practicing with the team.

Conference favorites that year? Take your pick: 1944 champ Ohio State or mighty Minnesota, with longtime coach Bernie Bierman back from Marine Corps duty. The dark horses? Michigan, Purdue, and the Hoosiers. One popular football magazine summed up Indiana's chances this way: "It is altogether possible that Indiana can cut quite a swath in the Big Ten title campaign. The Hoosiers don't meet Ohio State this fall, but must face Michigan, Northwestern, Illinois, Iowa, Minnesota, and Purdue in league games. If they get by Michigan on September 22, the Indiana boys might keep right on going. . . ."

Thursday morning, September 20, dawned cool and cloudy in Bloomington. The campus, sparsely populated with class registration still four days away, was all but deserted when the team climbed into the Buick Roadmasters provided for the trip to the Indianapolis train station. After an overnight stop at Fort Wayne, they would continue on to their Michigan headquarters in Jackson. As the caravan of autos slowly pulled away from the Indiana fieldhouse that morning, Indiana took its first step toward a championship.

David was about to meet Goliath.

—THE GAMES—

2

INDIANA AT MICHIGAN
SEPTEMBER 22

About thirty miles west of Ann Arbor, Bo and his "po' little boys" settled in at Jackson, Michigan, to await Saturday's game. They knew what they were up against. The night before, during a dinner held in their honor in Fort Wayne, the main speaker, a local sportswriter, had picked the Hoosiers to beat Michigan. He was the only one in the nation to do so. Michigan was favored by 10–14 points. Along with the starters and top reserves, included on the thirty-four-man traveling squad were freshmen Pat Kane, Jerry Morrical, Joe Postulka, Frances Oleksak, Nick Sebek, Tom Schwartz, Jackie Adams, Bill Bradley, Joe Gilliam, and John Gorkis. Others included sophomores Al Peterson, Leroy Stovall, Bob Harbison, Bob Miller, Bill Armstrong, and John Roper, and juniors Chet Sanders, John Kokos, and Art Lehman. Missing was Indiana's placekicker, Charlie Armstrong, who had informed Bo he was taking a job as a commercial pilot.

Since becoming a member of the Big Ten Conference in 1895, the University of Michigan had become the conference's football powerhouse. From 1901 to 1905, Michigan's "point-a-minute" teams went 55–1, scored 2,821 points to their opponents' 41, and trounced Stanford 49–0 in the first Rose Bowl game in Pasadena in 1901.

In the 1920s, Michigan continued its winning ways. From 1921 to 1924, legendary coach Fielding Yost's teams lost only once. In 1925, the Wolverines rolled up 227 points to opponents' 3. From 1930 to 1934 they won or tied for the conference title all four years. And even though a few lean years followed (Indiana beat Michigan in 1936), the arrival in 1937 of a great freshman class headed by All-American Tom Harmon led the Wolves quickly back to prominence. With these 1937 freshmen came a new coach, Herbert O. "Fritz" Crisler from Princeton University. Under Crisler, Michigan brought football to the height of perfection through the then-modern single-wing formation. By 1945 they were not only experimenting with the T-formation, but later that year introduced two-platoon football in a game against powerful Army.

Given its tradition, it is not surprising that Michigan, through its athletic directors and coaches, dictated many of the schedules and matchups in the conference. Indiana was not one of the favored teams. Michigan had played Indiana only twelve times and only once at Bloomington—in 1932. The Wolverines' 1945 schedule included six home games, two at neutral sites, and only two at their opponents' home fields—a decided advantage that wasn't lost on McMillin.

In the 1945 season, Crisler was attempting to build on the successes of 1943, when Michigan was conference co-champion, and 1944, when Ohio State scored in the waning minutes of the final game to win the title. Captain Joe Ponsatto returned from 1944 to run the Michigan offense. Ponsatto, the guiding genius of Michigan's power single-wing and its passing offense, had the experience to win games. Letterman Jack Weisenberger and talented freshman Dan Dworsky rounded out the backfield, along with Army veteran Bob Nussenbaum from 1944. The Wolverines may have been inexperienced along the front line, but they had plenty of firepower in the backfield. Against the Great Lakes Naval Training squad the previous Saturday, Dworsky and two other freshmen, Walt Teninga and Ed McNeil, scored three touchdowns in Michigan's 27–2 victory. Even though the Great Lakes team of 1945 wasn't as strong as its other wartime teams, any victory over a team coached by Paul Brown was significant. And of course there was the revenge factor for the Hoosiers' 20–0 win in 1944. That decisive win marked the first time the Wolverines had been held scoreless since 1941. Crisler and his team planned to halt the Hoosiers' winning streak over Michigan at one.

The coaching matchup was intriguing, too: Fritz Crisler versus Bo McMillin. Crisler was handsome, urbane, a former coach of the Princeton Tigers and a graduate of the University of Chicago. His "Champions of the West" would face an Indiana team coached by a man who seemed Crisler's perfect opposite. McMillin, slightly disheveled and prematurely gray, was a folksy guy from Texas by way of a small college in Kentucky. (Also, unlike the citified Crisler, Bo was a man who could run a pool table before you chalked your cue stick.)

McMillin had been at his poor-mouthing best prior to the

game. "We've got a great group of passers, yet I'll concede that among them there may not be a 'Hunchy' Hoernsmeyer,"—Bo's 1944 standout. And "pass receivers—if Don Hudson [star of the Green Bay Packers] were eligible, we could probably fit him in." He didn't stop: Michigan's "Walt Teninga is the best freshman in the conference. Linebacker and fullback are real worries for us." And so on. What McMillin didn't mention was Indiana's record in opening games—38–7–1. Of course, the Michigan Wolverines presented a stronger first-game challenge than the likes of DePauw, Rose Poly, or Fort Knox.

Arriving in Jackson after their overnight stop in Fort Wayne, the Hoosiers worked out at a nearby community park. That evening they attended a movie, retiring early to be ready for the next morning, when they would board buses for the thirty-minute ride to Ann Arbor. It was Bo's habit to arrive early so the team and coaches could take the field and test the playing surface. Before the bus trip, Bo pulled Taliaferro aside and asked him if he was superstitious. "Not really," the freshman back replied. Bo then asked if he would change jerseys, taking number 44. Taliaferro agreed, not knowing at the time that 44 was the number worn by two previous Indiana All-Americans—Vern Huffman and Billy Hillenbrand.

If Taliaferro had no cause to be awed by following in those footsteps, the rest of the team certainly felt intimidated when they entered enormous Michigan Stadium with a seating capacity of 84,401. As Indiana guard Bob Harbison recalled, "The long tunnel to the stadium playing field from the locker room seemed to end in a small circle of light too small for a midget to get through." Once out of the tunnel and onto the field, the stadium seemed immense, particularly for freshman end Tom Schwartz from Kokomo. "It was monstrous," he said. "Going out on that field the first time, I said to myself, 'What in the world am I doing here?' " Indiana halfback Dick Deranek remembered an incident that occurred prior to Indiana's 1944 game at Michigan, when the Hoosiers were also underdogs. "I'll never forget that," he said. "We were practicing before the game, fielding punts and so forth, and a ball rolled over to the Michigan side. I went to get it and one of the Michigan boys picked it up and tossed it to me and said, 'Here, I hope you guys can make a game of it today.' "

At two o'clock the game was under way and, after an exchange of punts, the Hoosiers began to dominate, gaining three first downs to none by Michigan. Superior line play by Indiana kept Michigan inside their forty-yard line for the first quarter. Meanwhile, Indiana's George Taliaferro played like anything but a freshman. He ran and passed Indiana to Michigan's nine-yard line, where quarterback Ben Raimondi threw to Kluszewski for a touchdown. Although Klu missed his extra point attempt, the Hoosiers led 6–0. In the second quarter, the Hoosiers scored again. From their own nineteen-yard line, Indiana backs raced to the Michigan forty-six. Raimondi then threw twenty-nine yards to Mel Groomes who, after making a circus catch, continued down the sideline for a touchdown. This time Kluszewski converted. At halftime, Indiana led 13–0, and it was obvious that Michigan's defense was troubled considerably by McMillin's "cockeyed T-" formation. But the Hoosiers had lost a vital cog in their front line. Twenty minutes into the game, center and linebacker Bob Meyer suffered a broken leg on a vicious crack-back block; he was on his way to a Michigan hospital.

Late in the third quarter, the Wolverines began to move. A punt rolled off the side of Taliaferro's foot and Michigan took advantage, marching forty-nine yards for a score. And near the end of the fourth quarter, Indiana began to have trouble covering Michigan's new spread formation. Michigan tailback Pete Elliot broke through the Indiana line for good yardage and then passed to another Michigan freshman, Bob Swanson, on Indiana's nine-yard line. But with just over a minute remaining, the Hoosier line stiffened. On fourth down the Michigan bench sent in a play designed to resemble a field goal attempt. But they took too much time, costing the Wolverines a five-yard penalty, and it didn't fool the Hoosiers in any case. Knowing three points wouldn't win the game, Kluszewski raced across the field from his end position to down Nussenbaum four yards shy of the goal line. It was over. The Hoosiers had passed their first test of 1945, winning 13–7 and, as in their 1944 encounter with Michigan, "making a game of it."

Obviously elated with the victory, Bo was quick to praise his Hoosier squad. He singled out Taliaferro's performance, saying: "He was a great running back today." Ever the teacher, McMillin also admitted: "We made some mistakes." He cited errors in execution on Taliaferro's two punts, tailback Bob Miller's intercepted pass, and Ravensberg's drop of a perfect pass. Still, he said, "everybody makes mistakes; I make them, too. I called a play on fourth down when I thought it was only third down."

Crisler, while modestly accepting blame for the fake field goal play ("I thought Indiana might feel we would be content with the consolation prize"), was less than gracious with McMillin's continued deprecation of his Hoosiers. According to McMillin's biographers, Charles Akers and John Carter, Crisler complained after the game to a reporter from the *Detroit Free Press* that "he wanted to hear no more expressions of grief over these tragic figures and, in fact, will refuse to meet Mr. McMillin either socially or otherwise until the next contest is decided."

Late that Saturday afternoon, when the wire services had posted all of the day's scores, quite a few fans and sportswriters had some doubts about the score from Ann Arbor. All at once, after decades of second-division finishes, the folksy but crafty gentleman from Bloomington and his "po' little boys" were making a run for the top.

Bo McMillin's "po' little boys" of '45 (left to right): (front row) Walther, Kane, Gingery, Postulka, Brossart, Sebek, Lysohir, Bradley, Oleksak, Moore, Erath, Horn, Gallant. (second row) Lesniak, Stovall, Gilliam, Harbison, C. Armstrong, W. Armstrong, Ciolli, Mihajlovich, Meyer, Adams, Miller, Kluszewski, Sfura. (third row) Rainge, Morrical, Deranek, Napolitan, Jones, Raimondi, Taliaferro, Ravensberg, Groomes, Stratton, Kokos, Weiss, Bauer, Novosel. (back row) Joseph, Peterson, Gorkis, Sowinski, Roper, Wright, Cannady, Guetzloff, Lehman, Smith, Deal, Sanders, Goldsberry, Schwartz. (Not pictured: Brown, Pihos, Buckner.)

Early in the opening game at Ann Arbor, Michigan, running back Walt Teninga returns a punt with Hoosier Jack Adams (center) and Bob Meyer in pursuit. This play was the last one of the season for Meyer, who broke his leg on the block thrown by the Wolverine in the foreground.

George Taliaferro, the fleet freshman who gave Michigan defenders all they could handle that day, steams off right tackle for five yards, thanks to blocking by Mel Groomes (left), Frank Ciolli and Ted Kluszewski (83).

With Nick Lysohir (33) following up the play, Mel Groomes hauls in a pass for Indiana's second touchdown, a twenty-nine-yard reception that gave the Hoosiers a 13-0 halftime lead.

3

INDIANA AT NORTHWESTERN
SEPTEMBER 29

On Tuesday, September 25, with their confidence growing thanks to their victory over Michigan, the Hoosiers began the week of practice for Saturday's game at Northwestern. Cannady and Deranek had been cleared to play, and kicker Charlie Armstrong had decided to give up his pilot's job and return to school and the squad. Still, Bo lamented the loss of center Bob Meyer, who had broken his leg early in the Michigan game. Consequently, center and fullback remained points of concern for McMillin, although Cannady could capably fill either position. Defensive drills that day were interrupted by a midday storm which also forced the university's freshman orientation indoors at the Union Alumni Hall. Fifteen hundred freshmen participated.

Early in the week, two familiar faces were conspicuous at the IU practice field. Coach McMillin had hinted at Monday's Downtown Quarterback Club meeting in Indianapolis that Indiana might have a couple of additions to the squad. Technically still in the service, Howard Brown and Pete Pihos had advised Bo they were on terminal leave from the Army but could enroll in school and play football for the Hoosiers that fall. McMillin and the team could hardly contain their enthusiasm. Pihos had been an All-America end for the Hoosiers in 1943, and Brown had started in the line for the Hoosiers before joining the service. Both had fought in the European Theater, and each had earned numerous battle stars. Brown was awarded the Purple Heart. Pihos was given a battlefield commission.

Wednesday morning, a half-hour before classes began at 8:30, new students were welcomed on the steps of the Student Building. That evening those freshmen still awake walked downtown to the Indiana Theatre to see Jack Benny in *The Horn Blows at Midnight*. But on Thursday, their attention turned toward football as the now-familiar parade of Buicks left the IU fieldhouse en route to Indianapolis. From there a train would transport the Hoosiers to Evanston, Illinois, where they would they would take the second step in their pursuit of a championship. However, this Saturday the Hoosiers would have some help from five guys named Pihos, Brown, Cannady, Deranek, and Armstrong.

Rain greeted the Hoosiers in Chicago. The forecast was for more of the same on Saturday. But when the players arrived at their Evanston headquarters, the famous Edgewater Beach Hotel, the gloomy weather was all but forgotten. "The thing I remember about the Northwestern game was that we stayed at the Edgewater Beach Hotel. Boy, that was nice," Tom Schwartz later recalled. A pale pink stucco structure located on the shores of Lake Michigan in the 5300 block of Sheridan Road, it had its own beach with a wooden walkway to the lake, romantically called "Beach Walk." The players could eat in the fabulous Marine Dining Room with its dance floor and starched white tablecloths or perhaps pause in front of the swanky Yacht Club with its "after-the-game" ambiance. Pretty good digs for a bunch of boys from southern Indiana.

On Friday night Bo turned the Edgewater into a practice field. Concerned about John Cannady's ability to center a wet ball, the ever-resourceful McMillin called his backs and Cannady to his hotel room. "Bo took some footballs and put them in the bathtub and then had me practice with a wet ball," Cannady recalled. "Do you believe that?"

The Hoosiers also witnessed another first that week. After Friday's practice at the stadium, Northwestern coach Lynn "Pappy" Waldorf entered the Hoosier locker room in a jocular mood. He and McMillin were old friends, although it was clearly unorthodox for a coach to visit an opposing locker room prior to a game. Pihos, keeping a straight face, demanded Waldorf's immediate departure, then the room erupted in laughter.

Since 1935, Northwestern football fortunes had been guided by Waldorf, a big, happy man who made friends easily. Pappy's coaching career closely paralleled McMillin's. When Bo left Kansas State following the 1933 season, he was succeeded by Waldorf, who promptly coached the Wildcats to their first Big 6 championship. This was enough to convince Northwestern that Waldorf was their man. His teams responded by finishing in the first division of the conference six times in seven years preceding World War II. In 1936 Northwestern won the conference championship.

And although 1942 and 1944 brought losing seasons, All-America quarterback Otto Graham led the 1943 Wildcats to six wins in eight games, losing only to nationally ranked Notre Dame and Michigan. Northwestern's proximity to Chicago and its fertile high school recruiting grounds had long kept Northwestern competitive, although in recent years the Wildcats hadn't been as successful as during the 1930s.

In the Wildcats' season opener at home the previous Saturday, back Dick Conners had rushed for ninety-nine yards to lead Northwestern to an 18–6 win over Iowa State. Still, 1945 looked to be a tough year for the Wildcats. Northwestern faced several squad defections and additions—much as Indiana and other teams confronted that year. Freshman participation was crucial, although some lettermen returned from a team that had lost nine games in 1944. True to the times, no player had more than two years' experience. The squad of seventy included civilians, 4Fs, V-12 service trainees, veterans and ROTC enrollees. Northwestern's fortunes for the year were hurt seriously by the absence of its usual array of naval trainees.

One of the few experienced backs on the squad was Conners, a bright spot in the Wildcats' 1944 season. Fullback Bill Travers and end Max Morris were V-12 trainees for the Wildcats. However, Waldorf was forced to use freshmen at five positions. By the end of the season, Captain Morris was good enough to be named the conference's outstanding player for 1945.

Unlike Michigan, Ohio State, and Minnesota, the Wildcats were frequent opponents for Indiana, meeting twenty-three times since the turn of the century. The Hoosiers had won only six of those games, including 1944's 14–7 victory at Evanston. Saturday's playground, Dyche Stadium, was erected in 1926. It was one of the many stadiums built during that decade to replace aging wooden structures. Seating capacity approached forty-five thousand, with a majority of the seats on the west side. Its location on Lake Michigan, coupled with the absence of seats in the end zones, made for many a seasonal surprise, particularly strong winds off the lake.

Proximity to Chicago made Wildcat games a media event. Bill Stern, America's most celebrated sportscaster, hung out his NBC banner from the press box, and Chicago's powerful station WGN was also on hand, with popular Midwest announcer John Harrington broadcasting "the week's top football game" on station WBBM. From Indianapolis came young Tom Carnegie and Larry Gordon for radio station WIRE.

The rain had ended before the 2 P.M. kickoff, but a strong wind still buffeted the thirty thousand fans in attendance and played havoc with anything airborne. "The wind was out of sight," recalled Indiana guard Bob Harbison. "You couldn't punt the ball beyond the line of scrimmage." Pihos, Cannady and Brown were on the sidelines for the start of the game, but would certainly play later. In their places, Bo used two freshmen: Francis Oleksak at center and Nick Lysohir at fullback along with dependable junior Frank Ciolli at guard.

Once the game was under way, the Hoosiers appeared confused by Northwestern's T-formation. Like McMillin, Waldorf was an advocate of the single-wing, but he had installed the T because he was blessed with good backfield speed, particularly in Conners. In the first fifteen minutes, Conners twice broke though Indiana's defense for long runs—fifty-one and sixty-four yards— but the Wildcats weren't able to score. However, it was Conners' fifty-one-yard run that moved the ball deep into Hoosier territory. Halted there, the Hoosiers were forced to punt. Taliaferro's kick was blocked by tackle Charlie Hagmann, and Northwestern's Stan Gorski fell on the ball in Indiana's end zone. The Wildcats led by a touchdown. McMillin immediately inserted Pihos and Brown into the game, but they didn't bring much offense with them right then. There was no more scoring on that windswept field until midway into the final quarter. It seemed Indiana's team of destiny was about to suffer an ignominious defeat to a green Northwestern squad that had been a two-touchdown underdog.

But with Indiana in possession of the football on its own forty-five-yard line and only five minutes remaining in the game, Pihos and the Hoosiers began to take charge. First, Kluszewski picked up four yards on an end-around play, and then Raimondi found Groomes open at the Wildcat thirty-six. Again, big Klu came lumbering around end; but this time he stopped behind the line of scrimmage and passed to Bob Ravensberg for a twenty-one-yard gain to the Northwestern fifteen.

On the next play, Pihos drifted out to the right and Raimondi found him with a pass at Northwestern's five-yard line. Purple-clad Wildcats swarmed the big fullback, but he was determined to score. He did, with three Northwestern tacklers hanging on.

Charlie Armstrong, who had been flying B-24s earlier that year and had been with the team less that a week, entered the game to attempt the important extra point. Frank Ciolli recalls the moment: "We were all standing on the sidelines; you could hear a few Hail Marys." But Armstrong's kick was true and the game was tied.

Back came the Wildcats to Indiana's thirty-five-yard line before Indiana forced them to give up the ball. With only ninety seconds left, the Hoosiers began a desperate drive that covered fifty-six yards. With sixteen seconds left, Raimondi found Mel Groomes with a pass, but Groomes was tackled on Northwestern's nine-yard line as time ran out. A 7–7 tie, but the Hoosiers were still undefeated.

Although Indiana had twelve first downs to Northwestern's ten, the Wildcats led in total offense, 290 to 235 yards. Taliaferro was effectively stopped, gaining only 56 yards on nineteen carries. Northwestern's Conners gained 158 yards for the afternoon.

It wasn't a celebratory squad that returned to Bloomington that evening. Northwestern had been referred to in one preseason magazine as "not a team of immense promise." That was charitable compared to another writer, who described the Wildcats' cause as "almost hopeless." But Pappy Waldorf was nobody's fool. His use of the T-formation, a deceptive and quick-starting offensive weapon, had befuddled Indiana early in the game. And the Hoosiers' week preceding Northwestern had been complicated by the reintegration of Pihos and Brown. Still, the defense had been stingy, and the Hoosiers moved the ball well late in the game.

"We pulled it out in the last quarter because of Pihos," Taliaferro recalled. "They had done such a good job of bottling me up that Pihos, Brown, Sowinski, Deal, Goldsberry and Cannady said: 'Let's go get them.' It was at this time I realized there was a nucleus of people on this team that were going to win."

The stylish cover of the Northwestern-Indiana program.

1946 *Arbutus*

George Taliaferro (44) turns to face disaster—his punt that had been blocked deep in Indiana territory by Wildcat tackle Charlie Hagmann (75). Northwestern's Stan Gorski (62) ran down the ball and fell on it in the end zone, giving the Wildcats a 6–0 lead.

1946 *Arbutus*

"Bullet Ben" Raimondi forsakes his hard-throwing ways on this play, lofting a soft pass to Taliaferro over a leaping Northwestern defender. Also in on the play are Bob Harbison (64), Bob Ravensberg (61), Alan Horn (50), John Goldsberry (78), Howard Brown (73) and Russ Deal (67).

1946 *Arbutus*

A trail of would-be tacklers in his wake, Pete Pihos stretches out in the Northwestern end zone. With time ticking down in the fourth quarter and the Hoosiers trailing 7–0, Pihos had gathered in a short pass from Raimondi and bulled his way in for the touchdown. That score, coupled with Charlie Armstrong's extra point, gave the Hoosiers a 7–7 tie.

—4—

INDIANA AT ILLINOIS
OCTOBER 6

For the third straight week, Indiana began preparations for a road game. This Saturday the Fighting Illini awaited at Champaign-Urbana.

Results of the Northwestern game were mixed. No, Indiana hadn't won, but since the Wildcats had outplayed them until the final quarter, a tie seemed more than the usual moral victory, especially since Pete Pihos and Howard Brown were among those who hadn't even had a full week of practice; Illinois wouldn't be so lucky. Also, Deranek's health had improved, and who should show up at practice on Monday but former coaches C. A. "Timmy" Temerario and Carl R. "Swede" Anderson, both just discharged from the service. Assistant coach Johnny Kovatch could finally concentrate on end play because, for the first time since 1941, Bo had a full coaching staff.

By Wednesday, October 3, with baseball's World Series under way between the Chicago Cubs and the Detroit Tigers, Bo led his squad through a spirited practice session concentrating on protecting the kicker. A lovely autumn day permitted McMillin to extend the workout until dusk engulfed Memorial Stadium. With forty-eight hours until kickoff, Taliaferro came up limping. His status for Saturday was uncertain. Meanwhile, Bo resolved two concerns as he moved Cannady to center and Pihos to fullback. Thursday brought the opening of basketball practice, with the center position a grave concern for coach Harry Good. (He had only to wait a couple of months for Tom Schwartz to report and resolve the problem.) That Friday, the Buick Roadmasters were once again fueled up and waiting at the IU fieldhouse. With a tie at Northwestern, this was a must win for Bo's boys; a loss would effectively take them out of contention for the conference crown.

Champaign-Urbana, two cities forever coupled by a hyphen, were collectively referred to as the home of the University of Illinois, but the main part of the university was located in Champaign. Whatever the location, the Hoosiers had trouble winning there. Their last victory over Illinois was in 1939. In 1944, an offensive battle at Illinois ended with the Illini and their fine halfback, Claude "Buddy" Young, winning 26–18. The Illini finished 1944 with a 5–4–1 record, but three of their losses were to Notre Dame, Michigan and Ohio State.

Succeeding legendary coach Bob Zuppke in 1942, Ray Elliot had proven himself a meticulous workman with a warm personality and outstanding qualities of leadership. He graduated from Illinois in 1932, having earned varsity letters in football and baseball, despite bad eyes and a self-supporting life-style. His 1944 team, employing variations of the T-formation, set a modern scoring record with 273 points in ten games. And they put up a magnificent battle in the next-to-last game against conference champion Ohio State at Cleveland Stadium before a crowd of 83,627. (With gasoline rationing in effect, one would assume they all rode the trolley!)

Illinois' 1945 record was 1–1, the victory coming in its first game, a 23–6 win over Pittsburgh at Illinois. The previous week Notre Dame had squeaked by the Illini 7–0 in a game the Illini could easily have won. Eddie Bray, Illinois' ace halfback, hurt his knee in that game and would not play against Indiana. Fullback George Bunjan, with a fractured finger, was doubtful. Eddie McGovern, slated to start the season, was still recuperating from surgery for appendicitis.

Lining up opposite the Hoosiers was a formidable offensive front line including former fullback Bill Heiss at left end and Jerry Russ at right end. Lou Agase and Bill Kolens, just returned from the service, were the tackles, and Wes Versen and Les Bingaman, the latter at 277 pounds, started at guard. Standout guard Larry Forst was unavailable, hospitalized on Wednesday for—you guessed it—appendicitis. At center was veteran Mac Wenskunas, all 6-2, 210 pounds' worth.

Quarterback Bill Butkovich, brother of Purdue's 1943 All-American Tony, would try to generate the offensive fireworks for Illinois. Jack Pierce and Tommy Zaborac, both freshmen, started at halfback. Two recent servicemen, tackle Gene Kwasniewski and end Wes Tregoning, were also sure to see action.

The University of Illinois, long one of the "haves" of the conference, presented a significant challenge to the Hoosiers' championship hopes. Before the loss of Bray and McGovern, they had been ranked among the best teams in the nation. And they had added incentive on Saturday: Their lettermen were to be honored at halftime; in particular, the twenty-eight Gold Star "I-Men" who had died for their country. The weather on Saturday was drab, with clouds hiding the sun most of the afternoon. Despite the opposition, only 25,173 fans filled Illinois' Memorial Stadium for the 2 P.M. kickoff. It had been a long six years since Indiana's 1939 victory.

George Taliaferro had shaken off his injury and was on the field for the Hoosiers as the game began. But neither team could mount a sustained offensive drive, and the first quarter closed with no score.

The second quarter belonged to the Hoosiers. Early in the period Bob Ravensberg intercepted a pass at the Illinois forty-seven. Two strong running plays by Mel Groomes and Ben Raimondi brought the ball to the Illini twenty-two. After a first down at the seventeen-yard line, the Hoosier attack faltered and they faced a fourth-down play at the Illinois fifteen.

The ball was snapped, and a big dog from the Illinois band ran onto the field just as Groomes passed to Ted Kluszewski for an apparent touchdown. Of course the play was declared dead and the touchdown nullified. But back came Raimondi on the next play. He found big Kluszewski at the back of the end zone — too far back, unfortunately; Klu had to step out of bounds to catch the ball. Undaunted, the Hoosiers were back before halftime to the Illinois eighteen-yard line, but several passes fell incomplete and the Illini regained possession.

It was a worried and disheartened Hoosier squad that walked to the dressing room. But after a few choice words from McMillin, the Hoosiers came on with a rush to start the second half. The teams exchanged punts following Illinois' kickoff. Then Indiana, aided by a good return of an Illinois punt, started from the Illini thirty-one and used the running of Groomes and Taliaferro to earn a first down on Illinois' four-yard line. But once again the IU offense stalled and Illinois took over. Stymied again by the Hoosiers' defense, the Illini booted to Dick Deranek at the Illinois thirty-eight, but the usually sure-handed back fumbled, and Illinois recovered. On the sideline, Bo stood up, stuck his hands into his pants pockets and began to pace. Another exchange of punts put the Hoosiers on their own forty-three-yard line as the third quarter ended. But not before an unnecessary-roughness penalty against Illinois gave the Hoosiers momentum. Raimondi passed to Groomes for eleven yards. Then Ravensberg caught two Raimondi passes to give the Hoosiers a first down on the Illini fifteen-yard line. Taliaferro then got five yards to the ten. Finally, with twelve minutes left in the game, Bullet Ben hit Kluszewski for a touchdown—and this time it counted, although Charlie Armstrong missed the extra point.

The Illini took Indiana's kickoff to their own forty-seven-yard line; but they stalled there and, facing a fourth-and-nineteen, prepared to punt. Trying to block the kick, an Indiana player roughed the punter. Instead of readying their offense, the Hoosiers found themselves back on defense at their own thirty-seven. On the next play, Stan Stasica, whom Deal had thrown for a loss on the previous third-down play, broke through the Hoosiers for a twenty-eight-yard gain. It was first and ten at Indiana's nine. But the Hoosiers held, with Deranek knocking down third- and fourth-down passes in the end zone. At this point, you could stick a fork in the Illini; they were done. Final score: Indiana 6, Illinois 0.

The exhausted Hoosiers filed off the field, still undefeated. Purpose, enthusiasm and perseverance had paid off. Once again, just as with Michigan and Northwestern, they had come back after disappointing setbacks on both sides of the ball. When they had to score, they did. When the opposition threatened, the defense held. Most of the starters had played nearly sixty minutes; McMillin had made only nine substitutions. Bo's boys never battled any harder than they did that murky fall afternoon at Illinois, and the statistics proved their dominance: fifteen first downs to eight for Illinois, 241 yards on offense to Illinois' 148.

Russ Deal recalls that afternoon: "We still weren't set as far as our team coming around and playing together, but we started to come together at the Illinois game." Frank Ciolli added: "I think the Northwestern game kind of woke us up and, not to be overconfident, we just knew we were going to win this ball game."

Finally it appeared Bo's championship team was coming together. Bring on Nebraska!

I

Men's Day

Illinois
Memorial Stadium

Illinois vs. Indiana

Saturday, October 6, 1945

Kick Off 2 p. m.   Price 25c

The Illinois-Indiana program cover touted "I-Men's Day" at Champaign-Urbana, a day set aside to honor the Illini lettermen, including those who had died in the war. The game was a fitting tribute, a hard-fought battle in which Indiana prevailed 6–0.

—5—
NEBRASKA AT INDIANA
OCTOBER 13

On Saturday evening, October 6, as the Buick Roadmasters slowly pulled into the parking spaces around the Indiana University fieldhouse, a small group of family and friends gathered in the early-autumn darkness. Arriving from Champaign-Urbana were the undefeated Indiana Hoosiers, 6–0 victors over the University of Illinois. It had been a rough afternoon, and the players quickly dispersed after receiving instructions from the coaching staff about Monday's practice times. Checking into Bloomington next weekend would be the Nebraska Cornhuskers. Finally, after three road games, the Hoosier fans would have an opportunity to see their team at home. Appropriately, it would be homecoming, that ancient college rite that has long enabled alumni and undergraduates to satisfy a common urge—to party.

Nebraska, once the football power of the midlands, had fallen on hard times. First-year coach George "Potsy" Clark had to depend on seventeen- and eighteen-year-old freshmen in 1945. But Clark had had a long and successful college career, beginning in Kansas in 1916 and including stops at Illinois, Michigan State, Kansas again, Minnesota, and Butler University in Indianapolis. He was better known, however, for his ten-year stint in the professional ranks. His Detroit Lions of 1935 were the National Professional Football champions.

Thus far in 1945 the Cornhuskers had only scored once in losing to Oklahoma and to Minnesota, and the Gophers had pummeled them 61–7. Only four lettermen were on the forty-man squad. Of two hundred Navy personnel on campus, only four made the varsity, and none was on the first team.

Despite Nebraska's recent troubles, the series between the two teams had thrilled fans many times since 1936. The Cornhuskers won three and tied two in the first five years, but the Hoosiers captured the next four games. Nebraska's 1940 team beat the Hoosiers 13–7, and then went on to play in the Rose Bowl. But beginning in 1941, Bo's brilliant tailback tandem of Billy Hillenbrand and Hunchy Hoernsmeyer handled the Cornhuskers with ease. In 1943 and 1944, Indiana scored 108 points in two wins over the 'Huskers.

As Bo and his boys awaited Nebraska, practices went on as usual. McMillin took nothing or no one for granted. On a bright and sunny Wednesday, he prepared his defense for Nebraska's expected aerial assault and mentioned Pat Kane, Tom Schwartz, and Lou Mihajlovich as standouts. He also praised his freshman running back from Rushville, Bill Bradley.

On Tuesday, the university honored alumnus Ernie Pyle, the famous war correspondent who had lost his life six months earlier on a remote island in the Pacific. By week's end it was difficult for the coaches and players to concentrate on football, what with dances, queen contests, the fall carnival and the arrival on campus of *Life* magazine and an MGM Hollywood film crew which planned to film the game. Even more distracting: The players had to be confident of victory. Even McMillin gave himself away by disclosing late in the week that Pihos, Kluszewski, and Taliaferro were to be kept out of the starting lineup because of minor bruises from the Illinois game. They would be replaced by Mihajlovich, Sebek, and Miller. As one scribe reported on game day, "Only the old-timers who see the ghost of former Nebraska gridiron greats have the pregame shakes."

Early Friday evening, the players joined the homecoming torchlight parade beginning on Phi Delt Hill. But by the time the Pow-Wow Dance started later in the evening, Bo had his boys tucked away. The next morning, as cars began jockeying for parking places around the stadium, it became obvious that a huge crowd would welcome home the team that stood alone atop the Big Ten standings. By the 2 P.M. kickoff, more than twenty thousand fans had jammed Memorial Stadium on this sun-kissed autumn afternoon. It was the second-largest crowd in the stadium's history, excluding Purdue games. Only a previous visit by the Irish of Notre Dame had outdrawn Indiana-Nebraska on this day.

The Hoosiers received the kickoff and promptly marched sixty-four yards to the Nebraska two-yard line, first and goal. But Nebraska held on downs, and even now one can imagine the ever-excitable McMillin quickly pulling the warm-up jackets off of Pihos, Kluszewski and Taliaferro. But the Hoosiers held, too, forcing the 'Huskers to punt out of the end zone. And, after Raimondi's forty-two-yard punt return, it became apparent that Nebraska lacked the experience to cope with McMillin's deceptive attack.

After Raimondi's run, Dick Deranek sliced between Nebraska's end and tackle for a touchdown. Indiana never looked back, even though they failed to score again until the second quarter. A blocked kick recovered by the Hoosiers led to a Pihos TD. A fumble by Nebraska halfback Mack Robinson was recovered by Allan Horn and led to a Mel Groomes touchdown. A TD strike from Raimondi to Ravensberg ended the half with the Hoosiers leading 27–0.

Halftime featured the usual collegiate festivities, with freshman Jean McKinney introduced as Indiana's homecoming queen. Since the Marching Hundred had been disbanded, the Hobart High School Marching Band presented a special performance.

Sophomore Bob Miller, a tailback from Chicago, had the crowd on its feet as he raced ninety-five yards for a touchdown with the opening kickoff of the second half. Miller, an outstanding prep halfback, had the misfortune to back up a couple of All-America tailbacks in Hoernsmeyer (1944) and Taliaferro (1945). But, like the rest of the reserves, Miller awaited his turn and was rewarded with some playing time—and the experience of being on a championship team.

The reserves continued the rout in the second half, with Jackie Adams and Bill Armstrong supplying the offensive power. A fumble recovery by Nick Sebek allowed Armstrong to score his second touchdown, and end Tom Schwartz returned an errant 'Husker pass thirty-five yards for the Hoosiers' last touchdown in the 54–14 victory. Bo had emptied his bench, and players who had practiced hard all season got their opportunity to play—reserves such as Big John Roper, Pat Kane, Leroy Stovall, Nick Lysohir, Don Jones, Bob Harbison, Chester Sanders, Joe Gilliam, Bill Bradley, Art Lehman, Al Peterson, John Gorkis, Bob Walther, Joe Postulka, and sophomore tackle Bob Joseph.

After the game, fans, players and students concluded homecoming week by attending the blanket hop at Alumni Hall. Some wandered to downtown Bloomington to party, others to visit the Princess Theater for a showing of *G.I. Joe*, which told the story of Ernie Pyle. Whatever their choice that beautiful fall evening, there was music in the air—Judy Garland's "On the Atchison, Topeka and the Santa Fe," "You Belong to My Heart," or Vaughn Monroe's "There, I've Said It Again."

The first postwar homecoming and a Hoosier victory: It couldn't get any better than that.

1946 *Arbutus*
Howard Brown (73) and Bob Ravensberg have Nebraska halfback
Mack Robinson sandwiched as Charlie Armstrong (72) rushes in to
add a little relish.

1946 *Arbutus*
Homecoming Queen Jean McKinney is crowned by Indiana Lieuten-
ant-Governor Richard James.

Life magazine

The members of Alpha Omicron Pi show that they support their Hoosiers from the bottom of their . . . well, their bottoms.

—6—

INDIANA AT IOWA

OCTOBER 20

The Associated Press college football rankings released October 16 reflected the results of Saturday's games. Mighty Army retained the number one spot, but in close pursuit were four teams from the Big Ten, including Ohio State, undefeated and ranked fourth; Minnesota, fifth; Purdue, ninth; and unbeaten Indiana eighth, just a few points behind the University of Pennsylvania. On Saturday, October 20, Purdue would visit Ohio State to fight for the Big Ten lead while Indiana headed to Iowa City to meet the Iowa Hawkeyes, whom Purdue had hammered 40–0 the week before.

Fully recovered from homecoming weekend and their trouncing of Nebraska, the Hoosiers had a spirited workout on Tuesday, concentrating on pass defense. Kluszewski rested some Nebraska bruises while sophomore Lou Mihajlovich stepped in at right end. By Thursday, McMillin pronounced his boys ready for Iowa. As usual he fretted over the "Hawkeye Jinx," which had started with Iowa's upset of Bo's great 1942 team and continued with a tie in 1943.

While the students were excited about the Hoosiers' success, campus life went on. Many students ventured to Smith Electric for alumnus Hoagy Carmichael's new record, *Hong Kong Blues.* Others saw Deanna Durbin in *Lady on a Train.* Those who realized that winter was near got their stadium boots at Marott's for $10.50.

As the thirty-six-man squad departed on Thursday afternoon, the dependable Buick Roadmasters were nowhere to be seen. Instead, Indiana traveled by train through Indianapolis and Chicago to its game headquarters at Cedar Rapids, Iowa. Although rail travel was much more comfortable than automobile, reserve guard Bob Harbison recalled that it was customary for the regulars to sleep in the lower berths, while subs were expected to climb into the uppers. Even though the cramped conditions cost the Hoosiers some sleep, the trip gave them an opportunity for togetherness and camaraderie. Questioned upon arrival, Bo lamented, "We're going to have a tough job on our hands Saturday afternoon." However, the Associated Press writer favored the Hoosiers, predicting: "The lightweight Hawkeyes will get some tremendous bumps."

While Iowa's football teams had had their moments of glory, generally the Hawkeyes shared the Hoosiers' role as a conference "have-not." The 1921 and 1922 teams were undefeated, but from 1923 to 1939, when Heisman Trophy winner Niles Kinnick led the Hawks to six wins in eight games, the football fortunes of Iowa were average at best. Bolstered by Marine and Naval trainees, the 1942 squad had shown promise, but losses to powerful Great Lakes and Michigan, coupled with defeats by Illinois and Minnesota, left the Hawkeyes with a 6–4 record. One of those victories had come at the expense of Bo and the Hoosiers, 14–13.

Thus far in 1945, Iowa had had a rough time. After defeating Berg AAF by one point in their opener, the Hawkeyes had been thrashed by Ohio State and Purdue. The remainder of the schedule included Notre Dame, Wisconsin, Illinois, Minnesota, Nebraska, and Indiana. The prospect for another victory in 1945 seemed dim indeed. In fact, given Iowa's 1945 personnel, one victory might satisfy interim coach Clem Crowe and his assistants. Of the thirty-five-member squad that had faced Purdue the previous Saturday, seventeen were service dischargees. The projected eleven starters against Indiana included five freshmen. Only twenty-six-year-old quarterback Ben Niles had earned a letter. Nonetheless, McMillin ran his squad through a workout shortly after their arrival on Friday. And on Saturday morning the Hoosier bus began its thirty-minute journey to Iowa City. Kluszewski had improved enough to start, but Bo still worried about the Hawkeye Jinx.

Iowa Stadium, built in 1929 at a cost of $500,000, was typical of stadiums of the day: large enough to handle most crowds but still not comparable to the palaces in Ann Arbor, Columbus, Champaign-Urbana, Minneapolis and Madison, Wisconsin. A crowd of 15,800 filed in on a warm, sunny day to witness this eighteenth game between the two teams. But apart from an Iowa rally that began late in the third quarter, the outcome was never in doubt. Indiana's experience and talent overwhelmed the Hawkeyes early as Indiana raced to a 40–0 lead at halftime. The

Hoosier line completely dominated the Iowa defense, and the Indiana backs gained 284 yards by halftime, led by the fleet Taliaferro. He had touchdown runs of sixty-three and seventy-four yards and racked up 102 yards on just eight carries. The first two Indiana touchdowns had little to do with Taliaferro or the offensive line, however. Both were defensive gems from Bob Ravensberg. First he scored after intercepting a pass on the Iowa 15. Later he followed up on Howard Brown's block of a Hawkeye punt by falling on the ball in the end zone. Scoring for the first half ended with a forty-three-yard jaunt by reserve back Bill Armstrong and a McMillin specialty—Dick Deranek on a forty-yard reverse around end.

In the second half, quarterback Raimondi took charge to pass for two scores, one for twenty-one yards to substitute end John Gorkis and a second to Deranek that covered sixty-three yards. Until late in the third quarter, the Indiana line had stopped every Iowa drive, but with Hoosier reserves flooding the field, the Hawks got back 20 points in the final quarter. Final score: 52–20. The statistics clearly showed Indiana superiority with 420 yards total offense. Iowa rushed for only 115 yards. Of the thirty-six members of the traveling squad, Bo used thirty-four, including Gorkis and Bill Armstrong, who both scored. The Hawkeye Jinx was dead—at least for a year.

Back on the Hoosier express heading for Bloomington, Bo surveyed his squad and found no serious injuries. Reports from Columbus indicated conference leader Ohio State had disappointed most of the seventy-three thousand fans in attendance, falling 35–13 to Purdue's brilliant backfield tandem. Illinois and Wisconsin had tied, Minnesota had topped Northwestern, and Michigan had enjoyed a week off following the Wolverines' 28–3 loss to top-ranked Army the previous week.

Back in Bloomington, popular band leader Les Brown crowned the lovely Madelyn Eastwood as Arbutus Queen at 3:15 Saturday afternoon. At Alumni Hall later that evening, the campus dance band played Les Brown's big hit of 1945, "Sentimental Journey." They played it not just for Les Brown, but for their unbeaten Hoosiers somewhere in the night between Iowa City and Bloomington.

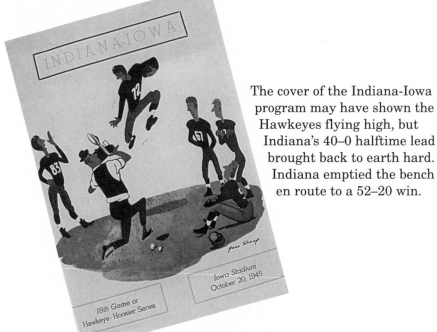

The cover of the Indiana-Iowa program may have shown the Hawkeyes flying high, but Indiana's 40–0 halftime lead brought back to earth hard. Indiana emptied the bench en route to a 52–20 win.

The Armstrong brothers, junior placekicker Charlie nearly wore out his right leg booting four points-after-touchdown and sophomore Bill, here holding, scored with a 43-yard touchdown run late in the first half.

−7−
TULSA AT INDIANA
OCTOBER 27

On October 26, a sunny Friday afternoon, a crowd began to gather around Bloomington's Graham Hotel to await the 3 P.M. arrival of the thirty-six-man traveling squad from Tulsa University, Indiana's opponent that Saturday. Coach Henry Frnka and his team had left the Tulsa train station Thursday evening to the cheers of five thousand fans. They stopped in Terre Haute the next morning and transferred to buses for the trip to Bloomington.

Saturday promised to be Indiana's toughest test. So far in 1945, the Hurricanes had demolished all five opponents, outscoring them 170–6. However, because of its weak schedule, Tulsa was only ranked fourteenth in the Associated Press poll. Indiana was rated eighth. Both teams were undefeated. Purdue had been elevated to the fourth spot.

When the buses from Terre Haute arrived, the crowd had swelled considerably. Reports from the Indiana ticket office indicated that five hundred Hurricane supporters would attend the game, and information from Bloomington's airport showed that an unusually large number of private planes were scheduled to land there before game time. As the Tulsa players left their buses and headed into the hotel, their size and strength were obvious to the locals. Prominent among the linemen was tackle Forrest Grigg at 290 pounds. Another standout was team captain C. B. Stanley, a twenty-five-year-old senior at 6-3, 215 pounds. Finally there was fullback Camp Wilson, a jut-jawed, rawboned 6-foot 1-inch, 200-pound senior who was thought by some to be better than Army's Doc Blanchard. Wilson had stunned the Orange Bowl crowd last New Year's Day with a ninety-five-yard kickoff return.

Frnka's record since 1941 made the Tulsa chief one of the best young coaches in the country. In his four and one-half seasons with the Hurricanes, Frnka's teams had lost only six games, tied two and had been to the Sun Bowl, the Sugar Bowl (twice), and the Orange Bowl. This relatively small school of seventeen hundred students was intent on competing in football with Alabama, Notre Dame and Michigan. And Frnka had the players in 1945, including twenty-five ex-servicemen, eleven of whom were new to the Tulsa campus. The squad had thirty-two lettermen on its roster.

As the Hurricanes hustled from downtown Bloomington for a late workout at Memorial Stadium, Tulsa supporters lamented the fact that their team was an underdog for only the second regular-season game in two years. Meanwhile, Bo McMillin and his coaches had scouted Tulsa well. They knew their Hoosiers would line up against a talented, experienced and deep team, one that, according to some rumors, included a few fellows who had played professional ball. But McMillin also recognized that his team was maturing and gaining confidence with each game. And he knew that Tulsa's opposition thus far had been less than Big Ten-caliber.

Bo worked the squad late on Tuesday, emphasizing kickoff coverage, run-backs and pass protection. Cannady and Kluszewski were expected to be ready for Saturday, but McMillin was still anxious. He had visited Bloomington's Downtown Kiwanis Club at noon and complained, "We're awfully thin. You see we have only about sixteen boys, and we should be three-deep to compete with Tulsa." Earlier in the week he'd told his team, "Unless we can rush [Tulsa passer J. R.] Boone, we're in trouble." Frnka was just as pessimistic. Before leaving Oklahoma, he avoided a prediction while complimenting the Hoosiers: "Indiana's backfield is plenty fast," and "Indiana's line? Boy, it can murder us."

On Wednesday, Raimondi, Taliaferro and Bob Miller took part in an aerial drill along with reserves Joe Gilliam and Nick Sebek. When Thursday's practice ended in the dusk of a brilliant fall day, Bo congratulated his defense and urged them to be ready for "one of the most rugged games ever held in Memorial Stadium."

The campus had come alive that Friday night in anticipation of Saturday's Dad's Day celebration and the upcoming gridiron clash. As the students celebrated date night by attending one of the many campus dances or perhaps strolling downtown to see *State Fair* at the Princess Theater, they knew that one of these two powerful teams would likely fall from the unbeaten ranks the next day.

Under a late-October sun, the crowd began to arrive Saturday morning, weaving in and out of traffic on Bloomington's narrow streets. Many fans carried portable radios, knowing that Tom Carnegie of Indianapolis station WIRE would be in the press box that day. They also were interested in other Big Ten games that day, including Michigan at Illinois, Ohio State at Minnesota, and Purdue at Northwestern, where the unbeaten Boilermakers were favored by eighteen to twenty-five points.

The Hoosiers followed their usual game day regimen: breakfast at 8 A.M., followed by a last-minute "skull session," then an 11 A.M. meal before arriving at the stadium locker room at noon. Unexpectedly, McMillin entered the dressing room and intimated that Tulsa's players might resent having to play against blacks. Before the Hoosiers took the field for pregame warm-ups, he warned them: "I don't want anybody to lose their temper." The Colonel remembered a practice field incident involving two Hoosier players—one white, the other black. Like a father teaching his sons a lesson, he'd let the pair mix it up a bit before having another coach separate them. "Had enough?" he asked. Both said they had, and practice resumed without further trouble. Back in the locker room after warm-ups, the boys dedicated the game— McMillin's hundredth—to their coach.

As captains Russ Deal of Indiana and C. B. Stanley of Tulsa met with Official Parke Carroll at midfield, the referee made it clear that no race-related incidents would be tolerated. Even fifty years after the fact, Deal could still recall the official's words: "Nothing unnecessary should happen. We're warning you."

The Hoosiers won the toss and elected to receive. Tulsa took the strong southwest wind. With their orange jerseys, white pants, and a big orange T on their helmets, the Tulsa players looked formidable across the green grass of Memorial Stadium. The Tulsa kicker moved forward, and Ravensberg returned his kick to the Indiana thirty-two-yard line. The game was on.

Neither team scored in the first quarter, but the action was furious. Tulsa fumbled on its second play from scrimmage, and Indiana recovered on the Tulsa twenty-seven. But three Hoosier passes fell incomplete, wasting a scoring opportunity. After an exchange of punts, Indiana regained possession. Taliaferro took a direct snap and ran with the ball. After the play was dead and Taliaferro still on the ground, Tulsa's Stanley jumped on top of the Gary freshman and kneed him. True to his word, the referee ejected Stanley and penalized Tulsa halfway to the goal line—a thirty-yard penalty in this case, thanks to 1945 rules (halfway to the goal or fifteen yards, whichever is greater). From there, the Hoosiers began to gain yardage. Raimondi spotted Kluszewski over the middle, and the big end got to Tulsa's six-yard line. But again the Hoosiers' passing attack faltered as the quarter ended.

Early in the second period, a pass from Groomes to Taliaferro moved the Hoosiers from their own thirty-eight-yard line to the Tulsa forty-six. After Taliaferro cut off tackle for nine yards, big Pete Pihos broke through the center of the Tulsa line and, when he reached the Tulsa twenty, alertly lateraled the ball to Ravensberg. The Raven raced down the field unmolested for a touchdown. After Charlie Armstrong added the extra point, Indiana led 7–0. A late Tulsa drive was stopped by a Raimondi interception on the Hoosier eighteen-yard line, and the half ended with no further scoring. The Hoosiers had held Tulsa to one first down.

In the locker room Indiana tried to prepare for thirty more minutes, but the time went by too quickly. Hoosiers' black runners, Taliaferro and Groomes, nursed numerous bruises and cuts inflicted by Hurricane tacklers. "They were beating the hell out of George and Mel," Pihos recalled. "Taliaferro more so because he carried the ball more often." (Given this game's racial overtones, it's interesting to note that just four days earlier, barrier-breaking baseball great Jackie Robinson had signed with the Brooklyn Dodgers.)

The second half began with Indiana again on the defensive. A Tulsa quick kick drove the Indiana squad deep into its own territory, and when Taliaferro attempted to run out of the end zone, he was tackled by Tulsa's Hardy Brown, giving the Hurricanes two points on a safety. Indiana 7, Tulsa 2.

The rest of the game was a heavyweight slugfest. Tulsa fumbled in its own territory, but Groomes fumbled it right back. Quarterback Boone threw a perfect pass to Indiana's goal line, but the receiver dropped the ball. As the minutes ticked by, the Hoosiers were bone-tired. The Hurricanes drove to the Indiana twenty, then fumbled; Ravensberg alertly picked up the ball and ran untouched into the Tulsa end zone. Unfortunately, the rules of the day did not permit an opponent's fumble to be advanced, so the ball was brought back to the point of the recovery. However, the play had given the ball back to Indiana, and had brought twenty thousand fans to their feet.

In the final minutes, Groomes was physically unable to return to the contest, so Dick Deranek replaced him, racing around end to Tulsa's thirty-eight. But the two teams were forced to exchange punts and, with forty seconds left, Pihos picked off a long Tulsa pass. It was over. Tulsa was no longer undefeated.

The game's defensive intensity was revealed in the statistics. Although Indiana gained 280 total yards to Tulsa's 85, the Hoosiers could complete only three passes. Tulsa completed one of fifteen. Three passes were intercepted, and the teams fumbled seven times. As fans streamed out of the stadium into the lengthening shadows, someone with a portable radio yelled, "Northwestern beat Purdue!" Indiana was now alone atop the Big Ten Conference.

In their locker room beneath the Memorial Stadium stands, the Indiana players stripped off their dirty uniforms. Many just sat, stunned by weariness after the sixty-minute battle. Indiana had used only nine substitutes. One of these, guard Frank Ciolli, said later: "That was the hardest-fought game I played in college." Pihos and Deal never came out of the game. Cannady, Taliaferro, Ravensberg, Brown, and Sowinski all played more than fifty minutes. But no serious injuries were noted—just a lot of bruises.

Taliaferro and John Cannady paid tribute to one hard-nosed Hurricane in particular. "They had a boy backing up the line that damn near killed everybody —Hardy Brown," said Cannady, Indiana's own superb linebacker. "I'll tell you, that Brown had a spring in him, and he hurt you." Brown—a 5-11, 180-pound linebacker from Fort Worth, Texas, who also did the Tulsa kicking— caused several of the Hoosier fumbles. "Hardy had developed a way of hitting people," Taliaferro recalled, "He didn't open his arms and tackle you, he locked his right arm against his chest and hit you with his shoulders." Brown went on to a successful pro career, where he continued his hard hitting.

As for the Tulsa Hurricanes, they lost only one more regular-season game in 1945—to arch rival Oklahoma A&M (now Oklahoma State), then fell to Georgia in the Oil Bowl.

Ted Kluszewski remembered this game some forty years later. Asked at a sports memorabilia show, the man who played 1,718 major league baseball games and hit 279 home runs replied, "Do I remember that game? You bet I do. The score was 7–2, I believe. And it was one of the toughest games I ever played in."

A tough game—and a sweet win for the Hoosiers.

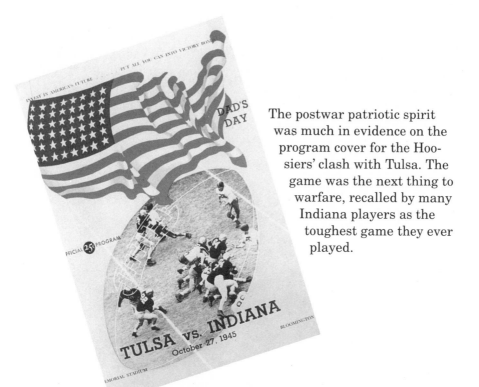

The postwar patriotic spirit was much in evidence on the program cover for the Hoosiers' clash with Tulsa. The game was the next thing to warfare, recalled by many Indiana players as the toughest game they ever played.

1946 *Arbutus*

Dick Deranek scoots around end with Tulsa's Camp Wilson ready to lunge at him and another Hurricane player in close pursuit.

(Both photos) 1946 *Arbutus*

The hard-hitting nature of the game is obvious in Howard Brown's helmet-jarring block on a Tulsa defender, springing Mel Groomes for a short gain. Time and again he was pummeled under a swarm of Tulsa defenders (below). As Pete Pihos recalled later, "They were beating the hell out of George (Taliaferro) and Mel."

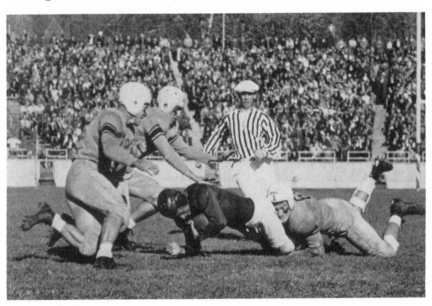

—8—
CORNELL COLLEGE AT INDIANA
NOVEMBER 3

On Wednesday, October 17, coach Bo McMillin had announced that tiny Cornell College of Mount Vernon, Iowa, would replace the Bunker Naval Air Station on the Hoosiers' home schedule for November 3. This game would come a week before the Hoosiers' critical visit to Minnesota. Although the Naval Air Station squad hadn't posed much of a threat to the Hoosiers' undefeated season, Cornell College was an even less demanding opponent. After all, it had only eighty-one male students. Coached by Walter Koch, Cornell was enjoying a good season in 1945, but had faced only smaller schools such as Iowa Wesleyan, Loras, Simpson, and Coe. Its only defeat so far had been to Loras, 19–7.

As always, the superstitious McMillin refused to admit publicly that he was confident of victory. This time, though, Bo's actions spoke volumes. He made plans to travel to Ann Arbor on Saturday to scout the Gophers as they faced Michigan, leaving assistant coach Carl "Swede" Anderson to serve as interim coach. Even the cautious McMillin knew a win was forthcoming.

After a well-deserved day off on Monday, Bo had the players back on the practice field Tuesday for what the papers reported as "a hard drill on defense against Cornell's diversified attack." That week, backfield speed was emphasized, with Nick Sebek, Don Jones, Jackie Adams, and Bill Armstrong receiving attention. The Hoosiers had moved up to number five in the national rankings after their Tulsa victory. Only Army, Notre Dame, Navy, and Alabama received more votes. Ohio State followed Indiana, with Michigan in tenth position and Purdue, Minnesota, and Northwestern all relegated to the second ten of the Associated Press weekly poll.

Shoe rationing had ended this week, to the cheers of students without cars—which was the vast majority, of course. And on Wednesday night, Halloween celebrations were common on campus. Also celebrating was John Ashton, who'd just been named dean of the School of Arts and Sciences.

With Bo traveling by train to see the Michigan-Minnesota game, Coach Anderson prepared the Hoosiers for a 1:30 kickoff on Saturday. Cornell had an excellent passer in Pat Rega, a stocky quarterback who had played two years for Notre Dame. Letterman Virgil Smith was usually on the receiving end of Rega's passes, and right halfback Glen Davidson gave the team a wide running threat.

As the dark-clad Cornell team lined up in Memorial Stadium for the opening kickoff, Anderson sent the Hoosiers' regular starting lineup onto the field. A bright, sunny day greeted an estimated six thousand fans, Indiana's smallest crowd of the year.

By the end of the first quarter, the Hoosiers had clearly established their dominance. Pihos scored following a pass from Raimondi, and Taliaferro scooted in from five yards out. The Hoosier linemen repeatedly pounded the inferior Cornell line, and that was enough for Anderson. In came the second team: Tom Schwartz and Lou Mihajlovich at ends; John Kokos, and Charlie Armstrong at tackle; Bob Harbison and Frank Ciolli at guard; Allan Horn at center; and Nick Sebek, Bob Miller, Dick Deranek, and Bill Armstrong in the backfield. Deranek started the second quarter with a twenty-seven-yard scoring dash around end. He appeared touchdown-bound again two minutes later, but fumbled turning the corner. The alert Leroy Stovall, leading Deranek's interference, scooped up the loose ball and ran fourteen yards for a score. (Though advancement of an opponent's fumble was prohibited, 1945 rules allowed a teammate's fumble to be advanced.)

After the half, Bill Armstrong and Deranek added touchdowns before the third team entered the fray. Even they responded, with Bill Buckner scoring on a two-yard run to cap a fifty-seven-yard, fourteen-play drive. A late touchdown accounted for all of Cornell's 6 points, but the Hoosiers had 46—and Anderson had used just that many players in the blowout. Before the final whistle, Pat Kane, Tom Schwartz, Wally Getz, George Dragus, Larry Napolitan and Al Peterson all saw action at the end position. At tackle: Art Lehman, Jim Hickman, Bob Joseph and Howard Wright. At guard: Bob Walther and Joe Postulka. At center: Nick Lysohir, Francis Oleksak and Tom Sfura played. And in the backfield: Joe Gilliam, Frank Bossart, Don Jones, Jackie Adams,

Bill Bradley, Simon Rainge, and Chet Sanders.

The Hoosiers rushed for 369 yards, holding Cornell to fifty-six. South Bend Central's Dick Deranek ran for 133 yards and three touchdowns—and it would've been four TDs except for the fumble which gave one to Stovall. Taliaferro only played ten minutes; Brown, Deal, Sowinski and Cannady only thirteen. Coach Anderson certainly didn't want anyone injured. Joe Sowinski recalled: "I think the starters were in and out the first half, and then we started the second half for a couple of minutes." From that point on, Anderson emptied the bench. Deranek summed it up: "We could have scored 150 points."

Elsewhere in the Big Ten that day, Purdue beat Pittsburgh 28–0, Michigan trounced Minnesota 26–0 in front of 85,132 fans (and Bo McMillin), Wisconsin handled Iowa 27–7, Great Lakes beat Illinois 12–6, and Ohio State edged Northwestern 16–14. The undefeated Hoosiers still held first place, but three teams— Ohio State, Purdue and Michigan—were in close pursuit with just one loss apiece.

Regrettably, one Hoosier had been injured in the Cornell game. Kicker Charlie Armstrong was hit from the side while attempting a point after touchdown. "They hit my bad leg," he recalled. "In fact, I could hardly walk." And with the Gophers only a week away, the Hoosiers needed a healthy Charlie Armstrong.

1946 *Arbutus*

Dick Deranek eludes several Cornell College tacklers on his way to a long gain. Deranek escaped often in this game, gaining 133 yards and scoring three touchdows.

—9—

INDIANA AT MINNESOTA
NOVEMBER 10

Tuesday morning, November 6, was a long day on the practice field for the unbeaten and highly ranked Hoosiers. Though still leading the Big Ten, Indiana faced a tough test in Minneapolis that Saturday—the mighty Minnesota Golden Gophers. Although they'd won their first four games convincingly, losses to Ohio State and Michigan the past two weeks had dimmed the Gophers' title hopes. But they were still a formidable foe, and McMillin knew it. Early in the week he moaned, "My, my, my, what power they've got—and nine seniors in the starting lineup. I'd just as soon play Michigan this Saturday instead of Minnesota, even if Michigan did beat them."

With excitement in the air, the week passed quickly on campus. On Tuesday, the university trustees announced that a School of Health, Education and Welfare had been approved. On Wednesday evening, those students contemptuous of early Thursday classes ventured downtown to see Ginger Rogers in *Weekend at the Waldorf*. And on Friday night Orrin Tucker's orchestra, sponsored by the Association of Women Students, heated up Alumni Hall until 1:30 A.M.

But it was Saturday's dance with the Gophers that remained on the minds of the Hoosier team. If nothing else, tradition favored Minnesota. Like Michigan, Illinois and Ohio State, Minnesota had been a conference powerhouse in football, particularly during the 1930s. Replacing Fritz Crisler as head coach in 1932, Bernie Bierman rode a ten-year wave of success at Minnesota that was unparalleled in conference history. During that period, Bierman's teams compiled a 63–12–5 record, posted five undefeated seasons, won five national championships and seven Big Ten titles and produced thirteen All-Americans. He used mostly homegrown talent—big, quick Swedes. Many experts still

consider the 1934 Minnesota team the greatest in college football history. And in 1941, Minnesota tailback Bruce Smith won
the Heisman Trophy.

Bierman left for the Marines after the Gophers' 1941 undefeated season, but had recently been discharged and was back at
the helm for '45. That alone was enough to put a few more gray
hairs on McMillin's mane. The teams had met forty-seven times
since 1906, with Minnesota holding a huge edge at 29–15–3. In
keeping with the skewed scheduling of the Big Ten powers, the
last game at Bloomington had been in 1927, and the Hoosiers'
last win was a 21–7 decision way back in 1920.

So it was an uneasy group of thirty-four Hoosiers who boarded
the train Thursday after an early-afternoon workout in sixty-
degree weather. Although kicker Charlie Armstrong still felt the
effects of the leg injury he suffered in the Cornell College game,
Bo decided at the last minute to include him on the traveling
squad. As the train headed north to Chicago for an overnight
stop, the weather began to cool. By Friday morning it was bit-
terly cold as the team settled on the train for the last leg of the
journey, an all-day ride to Minneapolis.

The trip gave the Hoosiers plenty of time to consider this
week's opponent. "It was very much on our minds," recalled Russ
Deal. "We knew we were going to have a tough ball game. This
was the big one—outside of Michigan. Sure, we'd play them one
game at a time, but we knew this was going to be a big ball game."
While contemplating the coming clash, the boys entertained themselves with card games during the trip, but they also became
more allied in their cause. "I think traveling by train like we did
made us closer," said guard Frank Ciolli. "We got to know one
another better."

As the train pulled into Minneapolis, the temperature was
fifteen degrees. It had snowed on Thursday, so the Hoosiers had
to abandon their plans for a 4 P.M. workout in the stadium and
were forced indoors at the Minnesota fieldhouse.

"Everybody up there was telling us we were going to get beat
because Bierman had never been beaten two weeks in a row,"
Charlie Armstrong recalled. "They were so sure." And there was
reason for optimism in the Gopher camp. Veteran players dominated their starting lineup, including quarterback Merlin Kispert,
halfback Bob Cates and fullback Vic Kulbitski, the last a third-
year ex-Marine at 210 pounds. Minnesota also featured Captain

Bob Fitch at left tackle, a throwback to the Viking teams of the 1930s. Preseason prognosticators had lauded Bierman and Minnesota. "The dopesters see the veteran-dominated Gophers stepping forth in high from the first kickoff and gathering unstoppable momentum as they go," said one fulsome writer for *Illustrated Football*. "Bierman's back, and that alone is enough to make the Gophers a feared factor in the Big Ten," said *Street and Smith College Football*.

On the train, McMillin said: "We're mentally ready, but I don't know how we will hold up physically. I think the kids will play a good game, and if we can keep our first string in long enough, we'll certainly have a chance." But Taliaferro had a slight injury, Goldsberry wasn't feeling too well, and Ravensberg was playing for the first time with the new teeth he needed to replace those lost in the Tulsa game. And in a close game, with points after touchdown crucial, Bo was worried about Armstrong's ability to kick with only one good leg.

By Saturday, the weather had improved somewhat. The sun was bright, and the tarpaulin had been removed from the field, giving the players some footing. However, a stiff wind was blowing from the southwest, making the temperature seem even more frigid. Kickoff was 2 P.M., and ABC was set to broadcast the game, with veteran Harry Wismer in the booth. A crowd of nearly forty-five thousand huddled in Memorial Stadium, awaiting the referee's whistle. The Indiana players huddled similarly on the sideline, their feet stuck in a straw-filled trench for warmth. Bo had some hand warmers, but the players were far warmer when they were in the game. The pregame workout had been delayed while the tarpaulin was being removed, so players loosened up in the end zone. Bo cautioned young Taliaferro to warm up well, reminding him that cold air can quickly sap a player's energy.

Indiana chose to receive, which gave the Gophers' kicker the early advantage of a stiff wind. As a result, Taliaferro had to retreat to the goal line for the opening kickoff. Gathering it in, he sidestepped several tacklers, got some key blocks and broke free. There was nothing in front of him but the Minnesota end zone, but the frigid wind and his still-cold muscles slowed him down. A Minnesota lineman caught him from behind at the Gophers' five-yard line. "I went right through those guys," Taliaferro recalled, "but when I got within twenty yards of the goal line, I could hardly move. I was positively moving in slow motion."

Taliaferro got the call on the very next play, but he fumbled and the Gophers recovered. "I was so tired, but in those days you played both ways," Taliaferro said. "So when the ball was spotted, I was in the huddle."

The fumble cost Indiana a scoring opportunity, but the Hoosier defense held and Raimondi returned a Gopher punt to the Minnesota forty-four-yard line. From this point, the Hoosier offense drove to the eleven, where an errant pass was intercepted in the end zone by Gopher Bob Kasper, who raced fifty-four yards before being caught from behind at the Indiana forty-six. After an exchange of punts, the Hoosiers finally scored on a Pihos-to-Taliaferro lateral with just over two minutes remaining in the quarter.

As the second period began, McMillin couldn't help but wonder what else could go wrong. With the Hoosiers' two early turnovers, the score could easily have been tied. But championship teams thrive on adversity, and the Hoosiers responded. Taliaferro brought the score to 14–0 with his second touchdown run, a twenty-two-yard sprint around end. But the Gophers weren't done. Two completed passes resulted in an apparent touchdown; however, Minnesota was caught holding and the ball was brought back. The frigid conditions made it tough just to hold the ball, let alone score. Indiana fumbled deep in its own territory, but Pihos got the ball back with an interception. He then fumbled, and the Gophers threatened again. On the next play, yet another turnover broke the game open in Indiana's favor. Taliaferro intercepted a Gopher pass and sped ninety yards for his third TD of the game. With the Hoosiers up 21–0, Bo began to substitute. Taliaferro's replacement, Bob Miller, quickly added another six points on a sixty-two-yard run. And just before the half, Bill Armstrong, Charlie's brother, intercepted a pass and gained good yardage on two subsequent runs before Pihos took it in for a touchdown. Announcers at other stadiums that day had to look twice before giving the halftime score from Minneapolis: Indiana 35, Minnesota 0.

The Hoosiers scored twice more in the third quarter: Dick Deranek, with an excellent block from reserve end Lou Mihajlovich, picked up thirty-five yards and then caught Miller's pass for a touchdown. Near the end of the quarter, Raimondi hit freshman end Tom Schwartz for a TD that almost didn't happen. The lanky Schwartz, an all-star high school basketball player, recalled that touchdown, just the second of his college career: "I'm sitting on the bench, keeping warm, thinking because this is Minnesota I'm not going to get in. So I got wrapped up with straw on my feet and blankets all around me. All at once, Bo yells: 'Schwartz, get out there!' Well, it took me a while to get everything off, and Bo yells again: 'If you can't get out there, forget it!' I said: 'I'll be there in a minute, Bo.'" With a forty-two-point lead, McMillin could afford to display a bit more patience, and Schwartz rewarded it with the game's final TD.

Indiana substitutes held their own in the fourth quarter, and the game ended at 49–0. It was the worst defeat in the proud history of Minnesota football and Indiana's first win over the Gophers in twenty-five years. More important, the Hoosiers remained undefeated. Statistics proved Indiana's dominance: a 12–4 margin in first downs and 367 yards in total offense to Minnesota's 114. The Gophers completed only five of fifteen passes, and the Hoosiers intercepted six. And the injured Charlie Armstrong? All he did was set a Hoosier record with seven points after touchdown in seven attempts—a record that stood for forty-nine years.

As the Hoosier express headed south out of Minneapolis that evening, Bo and his boys enjoyed a well-earned celebration. Despite adverse weather conditions, despite playing away from home, despite several early turnovers, they won—convincingly—because they were the better team. Kulbitski, Minnesota's big fullback, never got started. Linebackers Pihos and Cannady "just ate him up," said reserve Nick Sebek. One aspect of the Hoosiers' celebration proved to be a mistake, though. In honor of his touchdown, Tom Schwartz bought a bag of chocolate-covered almonds and proceeded to eat all of them. The imprudent freshman spent the rest of the trip in the bathroom. "But Mutt Deal and Howard Brown looked after me and took care of me," he recalled sheepishly.

During the trip, the Hoosiers learned that Purdue, Illinois, Ohio State and Northwestern all had won that day, but Michigan had fallen to Navy 33–7 at Baltimore. And in the game of the day, powerful Army had dominated Notre Dame, pounding the Irish 48–0 at New York's Yankee Stadium.

When the train pulled into Bloomington, a large crowd—and the Delta Upsilon fire truck—greeted the team and another celebration began. It had been a long time since Indiana had been accorded the respect they earned with their win at Minnesota. Some writers and columnists, particularly those from Minnesota, blamed the loss on the Gophers' disinterest. Don't believe it. This was one of Indiana football's finest hours. Bo McMillin had suffered eleven seasons of disappointment. If there were to be any rainbows at the end of this one, he didn't want them obscured by any cardboard clouds.

1946 *Arbutus*
With Lou Mihajlovich leading the way (right), Bob Miller looks upfield as he gathers steam for his 62-yard touchdown run on the frigid field at Minnesota. Miller, in the backfield for George Taliaferro after Indiana had raced to a 21-0 lead in the second quarter, scored the fourth of Indiana's seven TDs against the Gophers.

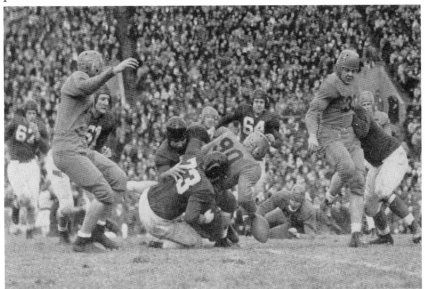

1946 *Arbutus*
Howard Brown (73) and Pete Pihos tackle a Gopher runner, forcing a fumble. Turn overs were common in this game, thanks to the icy temperatures and the stiff southwest wind.

−10−
INDIANA AT PITTSBURGH
NOVEMBER 17

Fourth-ranked Indiana—winners of six straight games, unbeaten and alone in first place in the Big Ten—had only two more games to win: Pittsburgh on November 17 and Purdue a week later. Despite Pitt's five losses in 1945, McMillin took no team for granted, particularly one that had played such a tough schedule. Besides Big Ten schools Illinois, Purdue and Ohio State, Pitt had also faced Notre Dame and Penn State. On the Hoosiers' practice field that week, none dared mention Purdue without incurring the Colonel's wrath. First and foremost—Pittsburgh at 1 P.M. Saturday.

Masterminding the Panthers again this year was nomadic Clark Shaughnessy, who had begun his coaching career in 1914. A brilliant strategist, Shaughnessy was famous from coast to coast as a coach who had popularized the T-formation. Success had followed him wherever he went—Tulane, Chicago, Stanford, Maryland—and now he had been chosen to restore Pittsburgh to the lofty status it had enjoyed under Hall of Fame coach Jock Sutherland. So far, Shaughnessy was still looking for an answer. His 1944 team had won four of nine games against inferior opposition. Reports from Pittsburgh, however, indicated the Panthers were up for this game, following a recent revolt over the prospects of the team and the ability of their coach. Two weeks earlier, Purdue had trounced Pittsburgh 28–0; the week after that, Ohio State's defending Big Ten champions had claimed a two-touchdown win on a rain-soaked field.

On Tuesday, with the end of war three months' past, the *Indiana Daily Student* heralded Secretary of State Cordell Hull's acceptance of the Nobel Peace Prize. And coincidentally, it was announced later that week that the United States would share its atomic secrets with the Russians if they would reciprocate and permit inspections. On Thursday afternoon, before the Hoo-siers boarded their train for Pittsburgh, they learned that guard Frank Ciolli had been chosen for the prestigious East-West New Year's Day game and that end Ted Kluszewski had been named national lineman of the week for his play against Minnesota. Somehow forgetting that this team was coming off the greatest game in the school's history in its win over the Gophers, some-one in the athletic department had failed to secure the appropri-ate number of train reservations for the trip to Pittsburgh. Only twenty-five Hoosiers left on Thursday; the eleven other mem-bers of the traveling squad had to wait until Friday evening. As a result, only a portion of the team was able to participate in a light practice Friday afternoon at Pitt Stadium. Not only did this disturb McMillin, the condition of the field was atrocious.

"There wasn't a blade of grass on that field," recalled George Taliaferro. Charlie Armstrong remembered Pittsburgh as a quag-mire. "It was hard even to find a place to set the ball," he said. Reserve end Tom Schwartz was even more depressed. "Pittsburgh had an old stadium," he recalled. "It was really in an old, dirty section of town. Because of the soot, everything was black. The stadium was terrible and the game day was terrible." Rain late Saturday morning darkened the mood even further. The squad worried not only about the loss of traction, but also about Raimondi's ability to throw a wet ball. Nonetheless, a game had to be played and won.

The Panther lineup that took the field for the opening kickoff had few stars, but it did have some bulk along the line. George Ranii, 5-11 and 210 pounds; Mike Roussos at 6-2 and 213 pounds; and the versatile John Kosh, a 6-foot, 180-pound former half-back who'd been moved to center. And despite Pitt's record, fleet left halfback Jimmy Joe Robinson had been a thorn in the side for Pitt's opponents.

The sportswriters had made Indiana an eighteen-to twenty-five-point favorite. The other important game this Saturday matched Purdue against the Wolverines at Ann Arbor. The win-ner would emerge with a chance to win the title if the Hoosiers faltered. Michigan was favored by three to ten points.

At 1 P.M., as the Panther kicker approached the ball, the mea-ger crowd of five thousand fans cheered in the rain, and eleven Hoosiers doggedly sank in the mud. Not surprisingly, the early part of the first quarter was scoreless as both teams adjusted to the muck that constituted Panther field. Indiana drove to the Pittsburgh fifteen-yard line, but that threat ended with a Raimondi fumble. The Hoosiers came back, aided by Taliaferro's interception of a Panther pass, but the Pittsburgh line stiffened, thwarting runs by Pihos and Taliaferro. On the next play, though, Bullet Ben held onto the ball long enough to throw it in the end zone to Ravensberg. The Raven clutched the wet ball and Hoosiers led 6–0. That score held until halftime, as the teams spent the rest of the half slugging it out on the soggy turf in the middle of the field. In the locker room during the break, the Hoosiers optimistically changed jerseys. "We stepped into the showers to wash the mud off and also change uniforms," Joe Sowinski recalled. "It didn't help. By the time we went back into the game, it was a mud ball."

Indiana asserted itself early in the third quarter. Goldsberry and Cannady blocked a Panther punt, and Kluszewski recovered on the Pittsburgh five-yard line. Pihos scored on his second try. Pitt, halted on downs after the ensuing kickoff, punted to the Hoosiers, who marched seventy yards through the slime for the final TD, again by Pihos. Pittsburgh's lone threat occurred in the fourth quarter, aided by a pass interference call. But Indiana held at its own nineteen, and the game mercifully ended with the score 19–0. The Hoosiers remained undefeated, thanks to Pihos' 113-yard effort on twenty-five carries; Taliaferro had slipped and slid for fifty-eight yards on fifteen tries. Besides his touchdown toss to Ravensberg, Raimondi was only able to throw three passes—all incomplete. Pitt did worse: eighteen attempted, five completed, three interceptions. The Panthers' running attack was held to only eighteen yards.

Bo had used fifteen reserves and so spared ten Hoosiers from action. Considering the game conditions, that was a blessing. Still, recollections of the Pitt game weren't all mud-encrusted. Mel Groomes recalled a personal battle with Pitt halfback Jimmy Joe Robinson: "Robinson had been running over everybody," Groomes said. "Early in the game, he ran a sweep around Ravensberg and I came up and tackled him for a loss. I didn't have to point my finger or stomp my feet, but I let him know he wasn't running around my end that day." Reserve Bob Harbison played that day, and his memories had nothing to do with football. Asked about the game fifty years later, he said: "It was interesting for us to see the Pittsburgh Tower of Learning, with most of the university in one building. And we always had a great time on those train rides."

Surely, everyone had a great time on the ride back to Indiana, though the coaching staff was probably looking ahead a bit. When he'd met McMillin in the midfield mud after the game in Pittsburgh, Panther Coach Shaughnessy had warned Bo: "Purdue is dangerous." Even so, the team and coaches were relieved to have the Pitt game behind them, knowing how easily a team can stumble by overlooking an opponent. Now there was no one to overlook. Only one hurdle remained.

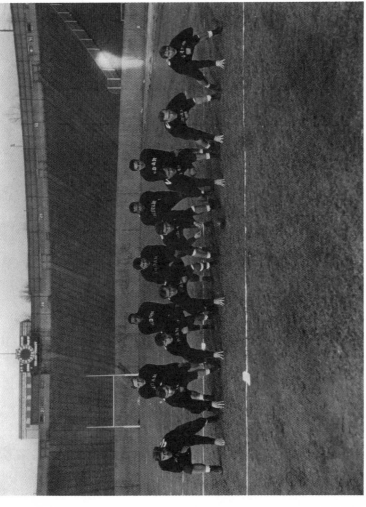

In a pre-game photo, before the field is trampled into a muddy quagmire, the Hoosier starters pose for posterity in Pitt Stadium. (From left, front row) Ted Kluszewski, Howard Brown, John Goldsberry, Joe Sowinski, John Cannady, Frank Ciolli, Russ Deal and Bob Ravensberg. (Back row) Dick Deranek, Mel Groomes, Pete Pihos, George Taliaferro and Ben Raimondi.

Bo McMillin and his hard-nosed ace, Pete Pihos, watch intently from the sidelines during the 1945 season. Pihos was Bo's workhorse in the sodden slugflest at Pitt, carrying the muddy ball 25 times for 113 yards and two touchdowns in the Hoosiers' 19–0 win.

Purdue at Indiana
November 24

Thanksgiving week in Bloomington had another important aspect in 1945. It was also Purdue week. On Saturday, the teams would wage their annual battle for the Old Oaken Bucket. And this battle would be the most important football game in Indiana University history. The Bucket, for twenty years the symbol of the rivalry between Indiana and Purdue, was placed on display (under ROTC protection) in the Union Building all that week. And on Tuesday night, hundreds of students paraded through the dark campus, carrying the remains of "Jawn Purdue," a stuffed dummy they buried with mock solemnity. Most students planned to leave for Thanksgiving vacation the next day.

The Hoosier players expected a hard week of practice, and they got it. Secret drills began on Monday and continued all week. They were geared to stopping the running of Purdue's Ed Cody, Bill Canfield, and Dave Shaw, along with passing of quarterback Bob DeMoss. Bo didn't like what he saw on Monday, so Tuesday he turned up the intensity and got results. Thursday, Thanksgiving Day, the Hoosiers ran through a stiff workout in the fieldhouse before adjourning to the Union Building for their turkey dinner. By now the campus was nearly deserted, but the players were too focused to be lonely. Bob Ravensberg remembers: "Who forgot a Purdue game? The minute you stepped on campus you found out you didn't like that school north of Bloomington on the Monon Railroad." Dick Deranek added: "We prepared for Purdue almost every week during the season. Oh yeah, it was a tough week." And Dixie Brown, Howard Brown's widow, recalled: "For Howard, the Purdue game was the season, no matter what season it was. That was just it."

On Friday, the hard work was over and the team tapered off with a light afternoon practice. By evening, as they tried to rest, the campus came alive again as fans began arriving for Saturday's game, along with reporters from thirty newspapers and broadcasters from ten radio stations. Temporary bleachers were installed at Memorial Stadium to accommodate forty-two hundred war veteran alumni of both schools.

Up the Monon tracks at West Lafayette, Purdue coach Cecil Isbell warned his squad about Indiana's passing attack, worried that his relatively small defensive backs would be unable to handle receivers because of the accurate arms of Raimondi and Taliaferro. But football fever at West Lafayette was reaching a peak. The team and coaches early Friday evening boarded buses for the short trip to Indianapolis. They would spend the night and leave for Bloomington at 9:30 Saturday morning. They had a police escort from Lafayette and to calm their nerves, they sang barbershop harmony.

The Purdue band and fans meanwhile boarded a special train for the trip south. Back on the West Lafayette campus, a huge Friday night pep rally had culminated in the cremation of "Miss Indiana," an effigy that had been lying in state at the Purdue Union Building.

Although the Big Ten standings had been analyzed many times that week, it was important to point out again that any of three teams could be conference champion by late afternoon Saturday. The Hoosiers controlled their own destiny: A win and the championship was theirs. But if Indiana fell, the winner of the Ohio State-Michigan game would ascend to the throne. Ohio State's conference record was 5–1; Michigan was 4–1; Indiana was 4–0–1.

The 1945 season had been a good one for the Boilermakers. They'd lost only to Northwestern and Michigan, and a win over Indiana would close Coach Isbell's second season at 8–2. One of the youngest head coaches in the country, Isbell had starred for the Boilermakers from 1935 through 1937, and then completed five years as a brilliant left halfback and field general for the professional Green Bay Packers. Isbell's version of the T-formation stressed speed and power. It had given Purdue fans plenty of excitement in 1945, producing an average of twenty-two points per game.

Leading the Purdue offense was Bob DeMoss, a gangly freshman from Dayton, Kentucky, who led the league in passing following the Ohio State game. Three days later, on October 23, the Purdue coaching staff had proudly predicted that DeMoss was bound to become the greatest passer in collegiate football history. Supporting DeMoss in the backfield were Captain Ed Cody, who led the conference in scoring, and Bill Canfield, who was second in scoring but led the league in total offense. Right halfback Dave Shaw, an outstanding freshman from Indianapolis, rounded out the Boilermaker backfield.

The Purdue line featured four lettermen, including All-American tackle Tom Hughes and several Marine trainees. Clearly, Purdue was to be feared. The oddsmakers had installed unbeaten Indiana as only a slight favorite. (The conservative sports editor of *The Indianapolis Star* had predicted a tie.)

Saturday dawned bright but cold—a perfect day for this clash of titans. The Purdue team arrived around 10:15 A.M., having spent Friday night at the Indianapolis Athletic Club. By late morning, the sun shone brilliantly in a cloudless sky, promising a pleasantly cool, late-November day. The crowd of about twenty-seven thousand began to arrive shortly before noon. A tarpaulin had covered the field for several days, so the stadium turf would be lightning-fast, and a dusting of snow had been swept beyond the end zones. The teams had met forty-six times, and Purdue held a narrow edge with twenty-four victories.

The stadium clock approached 1:30 P.M. as captains Deal and Cody met with the officials at midfield. Indiana won the toss and elected to receive. In the tiny and crowded pressbox that topped the north side of the stadium, NBC's Bill Stern prepared for his national broadcast while Tom Carnegie of WIRE in Indianapolis hoped he could forestall any calls of nature until the game ended as there was no rest room in the pressbox.

Purdue's Tom Hughes opened the Bucket battle by kicking with the wind to the Hoosiers' Kluszewski. The game was on. The Hoosiers' first drive stalled when Raimondi grounded a fourth-down pass, giving the Boilermakers the ball forty-five yards from Indiana's goal. But on fourth down, Cody dropped a DeMoss pass and Indiana took over on its own thirty-five. On their second possession, Indiana backs raced into Purdue territory, only to stop themselves with a penalty and three incomplete passes. Taliaferro punted into Purdue's end zone, and Purdue's Dave Shaw reciprocated a few minutes later with a long punt that Raimondi lost in the sun. First down Indiana on the Hoosiers' fifteen-yard line.

The second quarter nearly repeated the first. The momentum swung back and forth with neither team able to dent the end zone. Toward the end of the quarter, Purdue missed several scoring opportunities. Shaw recovered a Taliaferro fumble to put Purdue on the Indiana twenty-three, but Indiana's defense held as Taliaferro intercepted a fourth-down DeMoss pass in the end zone. A few plays later, the Hoosiers were forced to punt from that end zone, giving Purdue possession on the Hoosier forty-yard line. The Boilers drove, but Ravensberg's interception of another DeMoss pass at the Indiana one-yard line effectively ended a scoreless first half.

On the Indiana sideline, coach McMillin pulled his hat down further on his head, turned up his coat collar and headed to the dressing room under Memorial Stadium. All of the practices until dusk, the rain in Pittsburgh, the cold in Minnesota, the near-disasters at Michigan and Northwestern, the eleven years of frustration — it had all come down to the next thirty minutes of playing time.

The passage of fifty years has dimmed the Hoosiers' recollections of that fateful halftime. One player recalled a Rockne-esque speech by McMillin. Another, Bob Joseph, remembered nothing to set this locker-room speech apart from Bo's typically business-like routine: "He'd usually say: 'This is what we're lacking; this is our strength; and this is what we've got to do.' " It has been recorded that Bo grabbed Pete Pihos by the hand and led him away from the rest of the team to a separate room. And when the team prepared to leave the dressing room, tackle Bob Harbison recalled, "Pete just put his arm around Bo and said, 'Bo, don't worry, we'll get them this half.' "

Whatever was said or done in that room, it was McMillin's decision to rely more on his cockeyed-T formation that turned the tide in Indiana's favor. With the wind at their backs, the Hoosiers kicked off to start the second half. Shaw's return to the Purdue 28 was to no avail, and Indiana forced the Boilers to punt to the Indiana thirty-nine-yard line. Two plays later, Mel Groomes fumbled and Purdue recovered on its own forty-four. Shaw and Canfield took the ball as far as the Hoosier forty-one before Indiana forced a punt. It sailed out of bounds on the Indiana twenty-three, and the Hoosiers had a first down, seventy-seven yards from the Purdue goal.

All at once, Indiana clicked. The line opened huge holes: Pihos had nine yards; Groomes rambled for twenty-four yards and almost got away for a touchdown; Taliaferro went off tackle for ten yards; a Raimondi pass to Taliaferro took Indiana to the one-yard line. Purdue was looking for Pihos—and they got him. Pete was stopped the first time, but on his second plunge over guard, he scored.

Purdue unwisely ran the subsequent kickoff out of the end zone and got only as far as the six-yard line. A fumble followed, and the alert Kluszewski recovered on the one-yard line, setting up Pihos for his second touchdown. The momentum built in Indiana's favor. The Hoosier defense held after the ensuing kick-off, and Indiana took over on the Purdue thirty-nine. Taliaferro gained eight yards behind a wall of blockers as the third quarter ended: Indiana 13, Purdue 0.

McMillin's stomach was undoubtedly churning with fifteen minutes to play, particularly when his Hoosiers squandered a scoring chance early in the final quarter, stalling a drive on the Purdue twenty-two. Not only did they turn over the ball, they also lost Pihos with an injury. But Indiana's 4–4 defense, which had bottled up Purdue all afternoon, stopped the Boilermakers again. Indiana then began a drive at its own thirty-five, and behind the blocking of Goldsberry, Brown, Deal, Cannady and Sowinski, the Hoosier backs reached Purdue's thirty-nine-yard line. Bullet Ben then found Taliaferro all alone for a gain of twenty-four yards. On the next play, Taliaferro followed a Howard Brown block for ten more yards. Raimondi capped the drive with an end zone pass to Kluszewski. Although Armstrong's kick failed, Indiana led 19–0 with five minutes to go.

Purdue continued to pass in an attempt to overtake the Hoosiers, but DeMoss' underthrown toss was intercepted by Raimondi. Ben carried the ball to the Purdue thirty-four, aided by Kluszewski's block of George Mihal—a block that would be included in an NFL highlight film even today. Several minutes later the score became 26–0 as Raimondi threw a dart to reserve end Lou Mihajlovich for the final touchdown. The minute and a half that remained was highlighted by reserve tailback Bob Miller's twenty-yard jaunt around Purdue's right end—the final play of the game.

As the referee's gun sounded, a crowd gathered near the Indiana bench and, in the fading glow of this late-autumn afternoon, hoisted Bo McMillin on their shoulders. Everyone seemed to move in unison as the circle of well-wishers made its way to the Indiana dressing room. "I was still on crutches at the Purdue game, standing on the sideline, and I will never forget that scene," recalled Indiana center Bob Meyer. "I was just standing there as Bo was being carried off the field, and he leaned down, grabbed my arm and said: 'You're going to share in all the awards, also.' I had only played twenty minutes that season, but it was a great feeling and a great experience."

In the locker room, pandemonium reigned. The players jumped and shouted until Bo, tears in his eyes, silenced the crowd, "Boys, I want you to meet Chief Meyers, my high school coach at Fort Worth, Texas, and later my coach at Centre." Bo asked the Chief to speak to his "boys," but Meyers choked up after saying: "I'm prouder of Bo than anyone else in the world." So McMillin took over: "Boys, I've had a lot of athletic thrills in my life, but this is the greatest."

Congratulatory telegrams began to arrive: one from Arch Ward of the *Chicago Tribune*; one from Christy Walsh, agent to Babe Ruth and other athletes; from Michigan's Fritz Crisler; from baseball commissioner (and Bo's Kentucky buddy) "Happy" Chandler—even a one-word message from the popular country group the Hoosier Hot Shots: "Hurray!" Big Ten commissioner "Tug" Wilson, asked in the dressing room if the best team had won, yelled, "You bet!" IU President Herman Wells, long a supporter of Hoosier football, gave Bo a big hug, and their picture wound up in *Life* magazine a few weeks later. The young man who had been at Bo's side all season, assistant coach Johnny Kovatch, just sat on a stool and said to no one in particular: "Boy, am I tired." Bo's scout and close friend Paul "Pooch" Harrell, who had actually seen the Indiana team play for the first time this season, was in tears. It was he who, upon returning from scouting Purdue earlier in the week, had eased McMillin's worries about DeMoss's running. "Bo," Pooch said of DeMoss, "if he starts to run, I'll jump out of the stands and tackle him myself. He's that slow."

In the Purdue locker room, disappointment was almost palpable. No team had treated the Boilermakers this badly in 1945. Their powerful offense had generated only eighty-six yards, four first downs and one completed pass out of fourteen—and that for a loss. Fifty years later, affable quarterback Bob DeMoss, who went on to a successful career as a Purdue player and coach, recalled that every time he dropped back to pass he saw Goldsberry or Brown charging after him. And when he tried a bootleg play around end, there'd be Kluszewski, waiting with a big smile on his face.

As the crowd began to disperse, the campus came alive. Joe Sowinski headed back to his fraternity house to celebrate while Tom Schwartz met his family and headed north on State Road 37 back to Kokomo. Students made plans to meet later at Alumni Hall, where Eddie Oliver's band was to be featured at the Band Benefit Ball. And in the gathering darkness of Memorial Stadium, as the sportswriters teletyped their stories, longtime *Indianapolis News* sports editor Bill Fox recalled a little old man to his left in the pressbox. For years it had been this man's job to push the buttons on the electric scoreboard that revealed the downs and yardage. Face in hands, the old man was sobbing. And he wasn't alone.

A newspaper photographer captured the opening kickoff of the IU-Purdue game, played in jam-packed Memorial Stadium in Bloomington. The Boilermakers' Tom Hughes kicked short, and Ted Kluszewski fielded it to begin the historic contest.

Street and Smith Football Yearbook

Indiana's horseshoe-shaped stadium, with its twin towers standing at the open east end, held 27,000 fans on the day Purdue came calling—November 24, 1945. A dusting of snow had been swept into the end zones, and the afternoon was clear and cold.

1946 *Arbutus*

Mel Groomes breaks away from four Purdue defenders on his way to a long gain early in the second half.

Castle Films newsreel frame

McMillin's use of the innovative "Cockeyed-T" formation befuddled many defenses, including Purdue's. Here, back Mel Groomes is pulled back from the line at right, fullback Pete Pihos is directly behind quarterback Ben Raimondi, and halfback George Taliaferro is to Pihos' left.

How dear to my heart are the scenes
of my childhood,
When fond recollection presents
them to view!
The orchard, the meadow, the
deep-tangled wildwood,
And ev'ry loved spot which my
infancy knew.
The wide-spreading pond and
the mill that stood by it.
The bridge and the rock
where the cataract fell;
The cot of my father, the dairy
house nigh it,
And e'en the rude bucket that
hung in the well.
The old oaken bucket, the iron-
bound bucket,
The moss-covered bucket that
hung in the well.

—from *The Old Oaken Bucket*, by
Samuel Woodworth

1946 *Football Illustrated*

IU Alumni magazine

After gaining possession of the Bucket—and the Big Ten championship—with a 26-0 win over Purdue, Bo McMillin is surrounded in the
locker room by his "po' little boys." Was there ever a happier bunch,
or a more deserving one?

SPORTS

Life magazine

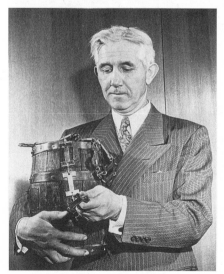

(Above) Hair disheveled and hat askew, Bo and Indiana University President Herman B Wells revel in the team's first-ever Big Ten title.

(Left) Later, with his coif only slightly improved, Bo shows off what he often called his "meal ticket," the Bucket.

-12-

CELEBRATIONS AND EXPLANATIONS

On Tuesday, November 27, after a one-day break to celebrate Indiana's first Big Ten football championship, university chimes called the students back to school at 8 A.M. The Big Ten title was an early Christmas present for McMillin, who called it his greatest thrill in sports. For students, faculty and alumni, it was the biggest victory in Hoosier football history.

Post-season honors were paid to players and coach. Ravensberg received first-team All-America recognition from three services. Pihos, Taliaferro and Brown made the second team, and Mutt Deal received third-team recognition from the American Football Coaches Association. Pihos, Taliaferro and Kluszewski all earned spots on the Associated Press All Big Ten team. Pihos was nominated for the Sullivan Award honoring the nation's outstanding amateur athlete and, had he won, the plate would have been full. But Army's Doc Blanchard was accorded that accolade.

Thanks to Indiana's stout defense in the Purdue game, Ben Raimondi topped Boilermaker Bob DeMoss as the conference's leading passer in 1945. DeMoss threw fourteen times against Indiana, but only completed one—for negative yardage. Taliaferro, the eighteen-year-old freshman, led the conference in total offense and placed second in scoring. As for McMillin, not only was he voted coach of the year by the American Football Coaches, he was also named Football Man of the Year by the Football Writers. For the soft-spoken Texan it was a fitting tribute.

On Thursday, November 29, the university held a late-afternoon convocation for the champions in the auditorium. Students hurried across campus in the twilight for a view of the Old Oaken Bucket and to hear President Wells: "We are here to pay tribute to those qualities of men which made victory possible—to skill, to devotion, to resourcefulness, to loyalty and to teamwork. . . ."

79

and athletic director Zora Clevenger: "A lot of us thought we would never see this in our lifetime."

After Captain Deal accepted the coveted "I" for attachment to the Bucket, Bo approached the front of the stage to thunderous applause. "I'm smart enough to know that it wasn't I alone who won that championship. Your praise sounds great, but it was the boys who won for you," he said. "I hope the championship will make them better men, better scholars, students better in every way possible, eager to be outstanding and to live up to their full capabilities."

On that partly cloudy and cool November day, the season formally ended, but another page in the year's celebration was yet to be turned. Before the month was out, a movement was afoot around the country, initiated by sportswriters, congressmen and fans, calling for a post-season game between number-one-ranked Army and the fourth-ranked Hoosiers. Number-two Alabama was already headed to the Rose Bowl, and Army had beaten number-three Navy. Why not a game between these two undefeated teams in Chicago's Soldier Field before 125,000 people—all for charity?

By December 4, the prospect of an Army-Indiana game was gaining momentum, particularly in Washington. However, General Eisenhower finally quelled the rising tide of telegrams and newspaper columns by denying the cadets permission. "The game is a good idea," he acknowledged, "but the cadets must prepare for midterm exams."

Obviously, this disappointed Hoosier fans, but the Indiana players had a more constrained view. Ben Raimondi doubted the game would be played, but thought the Hoosiers had a chance if it were. Newly elected 1946 captain Howard Brown was less enthusiastic, saying: "We're out of condition." Perhaps a bit of sanguine advice from Mel Groomes serves as a good epitaph for the 1945 season: "We'd better leave well enough alone."

For the record, the usual starting lineups for both teams were:

Army			Indiana	
LF	Dick Pitzer	195 lbs.	Bob Ravensberg	180 lbs.
LT	Dewitt Coulter	220 lbs.	Russ Deal	195 lbs.
LT	Art Gerometta	190 lbs.	Joe Sowinski	200 lbs.
C	Jim Enos	190 lbs.	John Cannady	210 lbs.
RG	John Green	190 lbs.	Howard Brown	200 lbs.
RT	Al Nemetz	191 lbs.	John Goldsberry	235 lbs.

RE ..... Hank Foldberg ..... 195 lbs.	Ted Kluszewski .... 205 lbs.
QB ..... Arnold Tucker ...... 175 lbs.	Ben Raimondi .... 180 lbs.
LHB .. Glenn Davis .... 170 lbs.	George Taliaferro .... 185 lbs.
RHB .. Herschel Fuson .... 215 lbs.	Mel Groomes .... 170 lbs.
FB ..... Felix Blanchard.... 205 lbs.	Pete Pihos .... 210 lbs.

Four of Army's starters—Coulter, Green, Davis, and Blanchard—were consensus All-Americans that year. Army's average total offense per game was 462.7 yards. Their running backs averaged 7.92 yards per carry. True, there were several patsies on their schedule, but the rest of their opposition had a combined record of 41–17–3—and Army had beaten them all. Perhaps Groomes was right . . . but then again, Bo and his boys had spent much of the season overcoming the odds.

How did they manage it? What made this team great?

Bo McMillin tried to answer that question just days after the Purdue win. At a Chicago luncheon on November 26, he thrilled an audience of seven hundred with reflections on the season and the team. Referring to the play of Pihos, Deal, and Brown, Bo said: "They were older, more mature. They were great players. But most of all, they inspired their younger teammates. They were the leaders. They wouldn't stand for players missing practice. They wouldn't stand for players being late for practice, to catch a train, or to bed. They wouldn't stand for a person breaking training. It was their inspiration among the freshmen and younger players as much as any other factor that carried the team through. . . ."

On the same day he made his Chicago speech, a column under Bo's byline appeared in *The Indianapolis News*. In it, he listed what he considered the two biggest factors in the team's success. First, he wrote, was team spirit. "Throughout the year our squad has been very considerate of one another." A player's mistake was always followed by three or four other players patting him on the back and offering encouragement. "Second," he said, "this Indiana football team had as much poise as any team I've ever had the privilege of seeing or coaching."

It's difficult to find a better or more timely assessment of a team's character than its own coach's comments just days after the season. But the players' views were just as cogent—even fifty years after their championship win. Pihos agreed that the players shared a strong desire to win, especially Brown, Deal and himself. But he also admitted: "We were just a little lucky, too." Mutt Deal saluted the coaching staff: "Bo didn't leave anything to chance. He just wouldn't let anything slip up on him." Tom Schwartz felt the older players blended well with the younger kids. But to George Taliaferro, the difference lay in four players: "Pihos, Cannady, Deal and Brown—they were men," he said. "Bo built everything artistically around those guys." Howard Brown's widow, Dixie, recalls the players' humility, praise that was echoed by Mel Groomes: "These guys were all so great, there wasn't any room for somebody to think they were the reason the team did so well," he said. Bob Meyer noted: "We were just all eager and willing to do anything they wanted us to do. . . . We were a team, a family. We loved to play, and Bo just kept saying: 'You can win.' He just kept motivating and motivating, and we just kept getting better."

Groomes took it even a step further: "This was just an unusual match of fellows coming to school at the same time and meshing like we did—just unbelievable. I don't think they will ever have another group like that at Indiana University."

—THE PLAYERS—

−13−
GEORGE TALIAFERRO

It was one of those muggy southern Indiana summer days where, absent a breeze, the heat was stifling. For freshmen football candidates at Indiana University it was business as usual that July day—one of many they'd spent since they arrived on campus in late June. This was merely another day in their quest to join the varsity next month in preparation for the 1945 season.

Under longtime coach Bo McMillin, Indiana's football fortunes had taken a huge step toward respectability since 1941. In 1944, the Hoosiers had gone 7–3 and had beaten the mighty Michigan Wolverines by three touchdowns at Ann Arbor. McMillin was guardedly optimistic that 1945 would offer Indiana an excellent chance to win the Big Ten championship. He expected thirteen lettermen back in August and, if the war ended by fall, some of his former players might return. Still, he knew he'd need some of his freshmen to play at least backup roles.

So, on this sweltering Thursday in July, McMillin and his staff decided to run a controlled scrimmage for the freshmen. Since their arrival, the freshmen had worked out without contact. Now with their pads on, Coach McMillin would see his boys play under game conditions. There was some talent on the squad, including Indiana state high school scoring champion Jackie Adams from Muncie and 6-foot, 235-pound lineman John Goldsberry from South Bend Adams. In a controlled scrimmage, the offense takes control of the ball on its own twenty-yard line; there are no punts or kickoffs.

In the backfield for the offense was a little-known freshman, George Taliaferro from all-black Gary Roosevelt High School. Gary was a long way from Bloomington—in more ways than one— and, in recruiting Taliaferro, McMillin had relied on the recommendation of Pete Rucinski, who was then coaching at East Chicago Roosevelt High School near Gary. With the ball on the twenty,

Bo called the "cockeyed 19" play—tailback off tackle. Taliaferro, at tailback, took the snap, bolted through the line, cut to his right and outraced the secondary eighty yards for a touchdown.

McMillin called the offensive and defensive teams together in the middle of the field and pointed out mistakes on both sides. He told the offense to run cockeyed 19 again. Again the kid from Gary ran eighty yards for a touchdown. The coach nonchalantly brought both teams to the center of the field and again went over missed assignments. He said nothing to Taliaferro. Apparently, he'd seen enough. He knew he had his 1945 tailback.

Taliaferro's enrollment at IU was certainly no sure thing. Both UCLA and Illinois had recruited him before he initially decided to enroll at North Carolina Century University, an all-black school. Meanwhile, as an eighteen-year-old, he was eligible for the draft. On the advice of a friend on the Gary draft board, he was told that, if he attended an in-state school, he would be deferred. This bit of advice, coupled with the contact with McMillin, set the stage for a long and fruitful relationship between Taliaferro and Indiana University.

Even so, Taliaferro's first few days on the Bloomington campus were humbling. First of all, black players stayed with black families; they weren't allowed to live on campus in those days. George was assigned to the home of John and Ruth Mays on Eighth Street. When greeted at the Mays home by fellow black Jackie Adams from Muncie, Taliaferro was asked, "Where are you from?" George responded, "Gary." "What all-state teams did you make?" Adams asked. "No, I didn't make any of those teams," George replied. That same day, Taliaferro got his first taste of big-time college football. "I'm lined up in the fieldhouse, waiting for my gear, when I notice the fellow in front of me, Goldsberry, at 6 feet and 235 pounds; Schwartz, at 6-5 and 210 pounds, was in back of me, and in back of Schwartz was Pat Kane at 6-3 or so. I said to myself, 'How in the world did I get invited down here?' " Later he told McMillin he felt overmatched, but Bo suggested he stay for a couple of weeks as the team would practice without contact for a while.

Fortunately, he stayed. "As it turned out," Taliaferro says, "I was the fastest guy on the team for my size, the best punter, and I threw the ball better than any of the freshman quarterbacks." His confidence grew day by day and he soon decided, "Maybe Coach McMillin knows a bit more about football than I do." Gaining that confidence early surely contributed to Taliaferro's quick start. His play against Michigan on September 22 was instrumental in Indiana's 13–7 win. And it's well to remember Pete Pihos, John Cannady, and Howard Brown weren't with the team at this time, and Dick Deranek played only sparingly. Had the Hoosiers not beaten Michigan, they would not have won the championship.

The next week, the Northwestern scouting reports highlighted Taliaferro's play against Michigan. As a result, the fleet tailback was targeted on almost every play. With Pihos and Brown back from the service for only a few days, the IU offense sputtered a bit. Still, the Hoosiers overcame an early Northwestern touchdown to score late in the game and earn a 7–7 tie.

A victory over Illinois the following week kept the Hoosiers undefeated, and they returned home the next Saturday to trounce Nebraska in Indiana's homecoming. The Iowa Hawkeyes then fell at Iowa City on October 20.

By this time, Taliaferro felt that the team was beginning to coalesce behind the on-field leadership of Pihos, Brown, Cannady and Deal. "It was almost like: 'I can block this guy; let's run here; let's fake over there,' and so on," Taliaferro recalled. After scoring a touchdown and while lining up for the kickoff, Deal or someone else would start shouting and patting each player on the shoulders, encouraging them.

A week later, in the game against Tulsa, Indiana came together to establish itself as one of the top teams in the country. Unfortunately, the game was marked by overzealous play by Tulsa, who lost their captain, C. B. Stanley, early in the game for roughing up Taliaferro. In fact, after a few plays, it was obvious that the Tulsa players didn't appreciate playing against blacks. Mel Groomes was also targeted, but not as much as Taliaferro. In the end the Hoosiers prevailed 7–2, in what Taliaferro calls "the best football game I ever played in."

After crushing Cornell College at Bloomington the next Saturday, the Hoosiers visited Minneapolis to play the Golden Gophers, one of the pre-season conference favorites. It didn't take long for Taliaferro to set the tone for the game. He ran back the opening kickoff ninety-five yards before being caught from behind on the five-yard line "I caught the ball right on our goal line and I ran right through those guys," Taliaferro recalls, "but when I got within twenty yards of the Minnesota goal line, I could hardly move, I was so cold." The quarterback called Taliaferro's number on the next play and he fumbled, but it didn't affect the outcome of the game. The Hoosiers won 49–0 that day, and Taliaferro crossed the goal line three times.

A soggy, cold win at Pittsburgh the next week set the stage for the championship game against Purdue. Practice that week wasn't much fun for the players. McMillin pushed the team hard and relied on superstition to keep his anxiety in check. "Bo had said he wasn't going to change his game suit or have it cleaned because of our tie with Northwestern." Taliaferro remembers. "It was a brown suit, and by the Purdue game it was as shiny as a dining room table. We can only assume he changed garments after the Hoosiers' 26–0 win gave McMillin his Big Ten title.

Post-season honors were numerous for the Hoosiers. Taliaferro, the freshman kid who three months earlier had felt he didn't belong on the team, was named Associated Press first team Big Ten and the league's best all-around offensive player. *The Sporting News* also made him a second team All-America selection.

But Taliaferro insists the Hoosiers' success had more to do with others than himself. "We had great leadership," he said. "Deal, Brown, Pihos, and Cannady, they were men. In my opinion, Pete Pihos was the greatest player to ever attend Indiana." The leadership from the sidelines was impressive too, Taliaferro says, referring to Bo McMillin as "just an incredible human being." He also admired Minnesota coach Bernie Bierman, who had praised Taliaferro's play in 1945.

One coach Taliaferro will not forget (or forgive) is Fritz Crisler of Michigan. Shortly after the 1945 season ended, Michigan learned that three of their fine freshmen players would be drafted. According to information given Taliaferro by these players, Crisler decided that, if Michigan was going to lose three outstanding freshmen, Indiana deserved to lose that Taliaferro kid who had run roughshod over the Wolverines in 1945. Crisler didn't take kindly to two consecutive losses to Michigan's country cousins. To ensure Taliaferro's absence, Crisler apparently contacted the regional draft board in Chicago, circumventing the Gary draft board, and demanded Taliaferro be drafted. As George was leaving Bloomington at the end of the first semester, he received orders to report to Fort Lee, Virginia, where he spent the next sixteen months. He was discharged on June 23, 1947.

The last two years of Taliaferro's career at IU were some-what discouraging. The 1947 team, Bo's last, managed to win five games, including a win over Purdue, but it was clear that team had less talent than its predecessors and lacked the depth needed to compete in two-platoon football. McMillin's departure for professional football in 1948 brought former McMillin assis-tant Clyde Smith to Indiana. Taliaferro recalls Smitty as "an extremely competent person. He loved what he was doing and he gave each of us his undivided attention." Sadly, after posting wins in the first two games of 1948, Indiana's lack of depth began to take its toll and the team lost all of its remaining games.

Even in the lean years, though, the time at IU was filled with memorable moments for Taliaferro. Over the dining room table in his suburban Bloomington home, he recalled the $1 pool that the Purdue players ran in one game. The pot was to go to the Boilermaker who knocked him out of the game. Taliaferro also remembered the roughness of every game against Notre Dame. In particular, he remembers a kid from South Bend, Casimir "Slug" Witucki, who chose Indiana over Notre Dame and was forced to pay the price, being pummeled by the Irish play after play in 1948. "They just kept running at him," Taliaferro recalled. "They butchered him." He also recalls his broken-field run in the 1947 Pittsburgh game at Bloomington, calling it his "greatest ever."

After graduation, Taliaferro enjoyed a seven-year professional football career. He played for the Los Angeles Dons of the old All American Conference; the New York Yankees; the Dallas Tex-ans; the Baltimore Colts; and finally, the Philadelphia Eagles, retiring at the end of the 1955 season. He made the Pro Bowl three years in a row after being named the conference rookie of the year in 1949. Taliaferro, and Hall of Fame player Chuck Bednarik were the last two players to play both offense and de-fense. Taliaferro was inducted into the College Football Hall of Fame on December 7, 1981.

After his pro career, Taliaferro returned to Baltimore in 1956, hoping to teach. When segregation of the Baltimore schools pre-vented his employment in white schools, he became a car sales-man and turned his attention to community service. Initially he was able to do some substitute teaching and later became em-ployed as a director of a community center sponsored by a Balti-more church. Subsequently, he obtained a master's degree while doing social work in Washington, D.C., and later became an executive with the Martin-Marietta Corporation. Taliaferro returned to his alma mater in 1972 as special assistant to IU President John Ryan, handling affirmative action for the university. He retired in 1992, and he and his wife Viola, whom he married in 1950, still live in Bloomington. They have four daughters and seven grandchildren.

And so, a relationship that began on a muggy July day in 1945 continues between George Taliaferro and Indiana University—a relationship that helped create the proudest moment in Indiana football history. And how would Taliaferro like to be remembered at his alma mater? Pausing for several minutes, he finally responds: "Nobody loved Indiana more than I did."

For tens of thousands of Indiana fans, the feeling was mutual.

–14–

BOB RAVENSBERG

Midway through Indiana's hard-fought victory over Tulsa, Hoosier end Bob Ravensberg was covering a Hoosier punt when the runner broke free from Brown and Kluszewski. Ravensberg caught the Tulsa player, but he also got the runner's helmet right in the mouth. Brought to the Hoosier bench bleeding, he spit out several teeth. George Taliaferro remembers the incident: "A dentist, Dr. Harry Leer, was on the bench and tried to get Ravensberg into the dressing room, but the Raven would have none of that. Blood was everywhere. All they did was clear his mouth out and give him some novocaine, then he raced back onto the field." Tough, resilient, and hard-nosed—that was Bob Ravensberg of Indiana.

He was also the Hoosiers' cheerleader, a screamer with a high-pitched voice that could be heard everywhere. Ravensberg was small for interior line play when he arrived in 1943, but what he lacked in physical presence, he made up for with quickness and intelligence. "He was good, he was quick. They said the guy was too small to play. Not true," says teammate Tom Schwartz. "He was probably the smallest man along the front line, but he was quick and smart," recalls kicker Charlie Armstrong. And the Raven had a sense of humor. Center Bob Meyer said: "Raven was a funny individual. Even serious, he always had a smile on his face. He was a great guy to be around." George Taliaferro recalled one incident which illustrated both the Raven's humor and his toughness. "Just prior to the Purdue game, Ravensberg took out his false front teeth and said to the squad: 'By God, we're going to kick their butts.' " The kid from northern Kentucky came to play.

Like several of his teammates, Ravensberg ended up at Indiana only after pursuing other alternatives. An all-state football player for Belleville (Kentucky) High School, his athletic ability helped him earn letters in basketball, track and baseball. Originally selecting the University of Alabama, he returned home after a few days at Tuscaloosa and decided to accept assignment in the Army Air Corps. While he waited, his parents and high school coach suggested he visit Indiana University in nearby Bloomington. Indiana's coach, Bo McMillin, had spoken at Ravensberg's high school sports banquet. The Cincinnati area had already produced another 1943 Hoosier recruit, Bob "Hunchy" Hoernsmeyer from Elder High.

After Ravensberg met McMillin and toured the campus, he quickly committed to Indiana. "I loved it. I realized I had found a home because there were so many nice people in Bloomington," he recalled. As for Bo, "He was one of the greatest men I've ever known. He taught me the difference between right and wrong and showed me that football and life were a lot alike. You get knocked down and you have to get up again." And so, in September 1943, Ravensberg joined an outstanding freshman squad at Indiana, a group that included Hoernsmeyer, John Cannady, Joe Sowinski and Frank Ciolli. Only five upperclassmen were available that year, and only two of those had earned letters in 1942. One was a junior named Pete Pihos.

In 1943, Ravensberg played outside or running guard on offense and one of six down linemen on defense. The young Hoosiers played well enough to post a 4–4–2 record that year, and all four losses were to service-laden teams: Great Lakes, Michigan, Northwestern and Purdue. Purdue and Michigan shared the conference title, while the sailors from Great Lakes and V-12 trainees at Northwestern were ranked among the top ten teams at season's end. Ravensberg was selected for the 1944 College All-Star Game in Chicago in August.

When McMillin greeted his 1944 squad, he discovered that Ravensberg, Sowinksi, Cannady, and Ciolli returned, along with five other lettermen and another outstanding freshman group that included Ted Kluszewski, Bob Meyer, Lou Mihajlovich, Bob Harbison, Dick Deranek, Bob Joseph, Abe Addams, and Harry "Chick" Jagade. Ravensberg had been deferred from service because of a 1943 football injury. Despite his size, he played left tackle for much of the season. Indiana game programs listed him at 6-feet-1, 174 pounds. Late in the 1944 season, McMillin decided his talents were best suited for end play, and there the Raven stayed for the remainder of his Hoosier career. Inspired by senior John Tavener, the team's All-America center, the 1944

Hoosiers finished 7–3 and were generally regarded as the best all-civilian team in the nation that year.

Ravensberg believes the foundation built during the 1943 and 1944 seasons made the Hoosiers' outstanding year possible. "The 1945 team was as good as any team I've ever had the privilege to play for. The team came together because Bo and his assistant coaches recruited student athletes during 1943 and 1944 who formed the nucleus for our 1945 championship."

For all of his athletic accomplishments, the 1945 season proved to be the quintessential season for Bob Ravensberg's career in sports. His offensive and defensive skills were much in evidence in every game. At Illinois, his pass interception led to the only score of the game. When Tulsa's defense threatened to stop an Indiana drive, it was the ever-alert Ravensberg who positioned himself to take a lateral from Pihos and run for the touchdown that won the game for Indiana. At Pittsburgh, with Raimondi's passing hampered by the sloppy conditions, Ravensberg caught the wet ball for the Hoosiers' first touchdown. With Purdue driving late in a scoreless first half, it was the Raven who intercepted a Boilermaker pass in front of the Hoosier goal line, ending the threat and the half. Of all the Hoosier heroes of 1945, only Ravensberg received first-team All-America recognition.

After spending 1946 in the Army, Ravensberg returned to campus in 1947, McMillin's last year. It was a bittersweet season for the Raven, but he played hard, as always, and Indiana won five of nine games. And his football career didn't end after the 1947 Purdue game. He went on to play two years with the professional Chicago Cardinals, helping them win the National Football League Western Division title in 1948. In 1950 he returned to his alma mater to assist IU coach Clyde Smith.

In 1958, after several years in the sale of building supplies, he formed his own interior-building-products firm, Ravensberg Inc., which continues today under the direction of his son, William. Bob and his wife, Sally, also have another son, Bob, an Indianapolis stockbroker. True to his university, Ravensberg has been chairman of the Howard Brown Endowment for the Indiana University Varsity Club and served as president of the university's Alumni Association.

From Belleville, Kentucky, a town of only nineteen hundred, to Indiana University, a Big Ten championship, All-America honors and a successful business career, the Raven has excelled at every level and encouraged his teammates to do the same. "When he returned that autumn of 1945, he was sure we would win," remembers George Taliaferro.

"It was fun," Ravensberg recalls. "When you win, baby, it's always fun."

—15—

BEN RAIMONDI

A few days before the Hoosiers' October 6 game at Illinois, the chief Illini scout, Leo Johnson, was asked what he feared most from the Indiana squad. The answer was Ben Raimondi, a strong-armed quarterback Johnson called "one of the best passers of the year."

Even at 5-foot-10 and 180 pounds, as he was listed in the Indiana press guide, Ben Raimondi was less than intimidating physically. And when measured correctly at 5-foot-9 and 170 pounds, he was downright small for a Big Ten back. But he could pass. He'd proven that through three years of varsity football at Erasmus High School in Brooklyn, the same school that produced All-American Sid Luckman of Columbia University and the Chicago Bears. As an Erasmus quarterback, Raimondi was selected to New York all-city and all-state teams. While he played quarterback, Erasmus never lost a game.

In 1943, Raimondi attended William and Mary College in Williamsburg, Virginia. However, before the next fall, he ended up in Bloomington, thanks to a recommendation to McMillin from longtime Columbia University coach Lou Little. "Bo utilized a passing game, and Coach Little thought I would fit right in," recalled Raimondi. Aided by the benevolent McMillin, whom Raimondi recalls as a father figure, Ben adapted quickly to the tiny college town in rural Indiana, even though it was a long way from the hustle and bustle of Brooklyn.

Eligible to play immediately, Raimondi spent the 1944 season as a backup to Bob Hoernsmeyer, Indiana's star tailback. Although his playing time was limited that year, he learned Bo's system during practices and applied those lessons when he did see game action.

In the spring of 1945, Raimondi broke his shoulder and was

unable to throw for two months. At times, his status for 1945 was questionable. But the toughness and tenacity he had acquired in 1944 helped him get in shape in time to play in September. That was critical for Indiana; McMillin planned to integrate the T-formation into his offensive scheme for 1945, and that demanded a passing quarterback. Raimondi was ready. Teammate Bob Meyer recalled that, in 1944, "he came in and wasn't doing too well because we were basically playing a single-wing, and he was not that good of a runner. But in 1945, Bo finally succumbed to a version of the T-formation, and Bennie then became our main passer. He was pretty accurate. Ben came into his own at this time and played safety on defense."

It didn't take long for Raimondi to establish himself in game action that fall. Although McMillin lamented the lack of anyone to step forward in preseason practice, it was Raimondi who was on the field for the opening kickoff at Michigan Stadium on September 22. In the first quarter at Ann Arbor, he found Kluszewski open over the middle for Indiana's first touchdown. And before halftime he caught Mel Groomes racing down the sideline for a fifty-four-yard touchdown pass. Then, at Northwestern, Raimondi and Pihos combined on a fifteen-yard pass play for the tying touchdown. The next week, at Illinois, after the disappointment of having a touchdown called back in the first half, "Bullet Ben" came back late in the game to hit big Ted Kluszewski for the winning score. "The defender was all over Kluszewski," Raimondi later recalled, "so I threw the ball out of the reach of both of them, but Kluszewski's big hand came out of the tangle of bodies and caught the ball for the touchdown." It was Raimondi's strong arm then, as much as anything, that had kept the Hoosiers undefeated in their first three games and given them time to solidify as a team. In the season finale against Purdue, he helped assure the championship by tossing two touchdown passes, and even intercepted a pass late in the game from his safety position on defense. Recalling the interception, Raimondi admitted he took a chance with the Hoosiers ahead 19–0. The Purdue receiver was the fastest man on their squad and Raimondi later admitted that, had he failed to pick off the pass, he never could have caught him.

Raimondi finished the season as the Big Ten's best passer with thirty-five completions in eighty-three attempts, twelve touchdowns and 593 total yards. Just as important, he surrendered only three interceptions. Ben was from Erasmus High School and tutored by Sid Luckman, Mel Groomes recalls. "Ben was wonderful, very open. He would ask me, 'Mel, do you think you can get open?' and I would say, 'Yeah, I can.' And he said, 'Well, it's coming to you.' He was real smart—very resourceful and easy to get along with."

Raimondi's last year, 1946, was disappointing for Hoosier players and fans. The Rose Bowl pact between the Big Ten and Pacific Coast Conference champions was signed that year in September, which automatically sent the 1946 Big Ten champs to Pasadena on New Year's Day 1947. It would have been a fitting tribute to the 1945 squad, most of whom returned for the 1946 season. But it was not to be. Although the Hoosiers beat Illinois, the eventual champion, their powerful offense was shut down completely against Michigan and Iowa.

Despite the team's woes, though, Raimondi's individual performance was brilliant. He threw for nearly one thousand yards, completing 54 percent of his passes. And Bullet Ben was rewarded for his efficiency. The first accolade came from the Associated Press, which named Raimondi a second team All-America player for 1946. Ranking ahead of him for first-team honors was a youngster named Johnny Lujack from Notre Dame. The second reward was more tangible:

"New York City, January 24 (United Press)—Ben Raimondi, quarterback and forward passing star of Indiana University Hoosiers, signed a three-year contract today to play football with the New York Yankees of the All-American Conference. Raimondi, a Brooklyn-born youngster who was a local prep school sensation, was the third-ranking passer in the nation last season, completing 74 out of 138 forward passes attempted for a total of 956 yards." (It was also reported that he would be the highest-paid player on the Yankees roster, earning forty thousand dollars for the next three years, including a handsome signing bonus.)

At New York, Raimondi's teammates included two old rivals from the Big Ten, Buddy Young from Illinois and Dick Barwegan from Purdue. And although he made his professional debut as the Yankees' starting quarterback, his skills were not ultimately transferable to the professional ranks. After an abbreviated pro career, he became a salesman. But his real love was teaching and, in 1966, he began a rewarding career as a high school teacher in the New York City schools, retiring after twenty-five years in 1991.

As his "Bullet Ben" moniker indicated, part of Raimondi's success resulted from the velocity of his passes. "He loved to throw the ball, and he was a great passer," reserve end Tom Schwartz recalled. "He would throw about as hard as he could at you, but always on the numbers."

From September 1945, when he led the Hoosiers out of the huddle for the first play against Michigan, until late November 1946, when he walked off the field after the Hoosiers' third straight win over arch rival Purdue, Ben Raimondi was a winner. He was far from the biggest man on the squad; in fact, he often was forced to jump in the air when passing so he could see the field. But the little guy from Flatbush did what he was asked to—pass. And he did it well, completing 108 passes in 218 attempts for 1,564 yards and 18 touchdowns in two years at Indiana.

Asked how he would like to be remembered, Raimondi replied: "As one of the hardest-working players on the team and the guy who introduced the bullet pass." George Taliaferro said of his old backfield mate: "He was as good a pure passer as anybody I have ever seen. Ben Raimondi loved to play quarterback; he loved to throw the ball. He thought of himself as an artist with a football."

—16—
FRANK CIOLLI

The size of the freshmen recruited by Bo McMillin during the years he was building his 1945 championship team would usually bring a smile to the Colonel's weathered face. Physical specimens like John Goldsberry, Ted Kluszewski and John Cannady were only a few of the Adonises who graced the campus beginning in 1943. Freshman guard Frank Ciolli from the Youngstown suburb of Campbell, Ohio, was an exception. Ciolli initially joined the Merchant Marine following high school graduation in 1943, but a scarred eardrum sent him home after six weeks. Brought to McMillin's attention by his high school coach, a player for Bo at Geneva College, Ciolli then accepted McMillin's invitation to join the Hoosiers.

Ciolli's arrival at Indiana ("the most beautiful campus I ever saw") and his first meeting with McMillin must have startled the wizened coach a bit. Ciolli stood only 5 feet 8 inches tall and weighed just 165 pounds. But McMillin knew that size was only one factor in assessing a player's worth. And if Bo harbored any doubts, Ciolli had none about the drawling, personable McMillin. "I felt there was no greater coach than Bo at that time," he recalled.

Playing enough to earn a letter in 1943, Ciolli and all of the great freshmen of that year gained valuable experience while helping the Hoosiers through a respectable season. By 1944, Ciolli had moved into the starting lineup at right guard, flanked by fellow sophomore Joe Sowinski at tackle and freshman Ted Kluszewski at end. The team won seven of ten games.

As he prepared himself for the 1945 season, Ciolli had a premonition: "That year you just had a feeling that we weren't going to lose any games. At practice and everywhere else, we felt this was our year. We knew we were going to win every ball game."

Lining up at left guard opposite Ciolli in the opening game at Michigan was seventeen-year-old Michigan guard Dominic Tomasi at 5-10, 180 pounds. The freshman from Flint, Michigan, had his hands full that afternoon with his shorter, lighter counterpart, and the Hoosier line outplayed and dominated the Wolverines. Ciolli had veterans Russ Deal and Bob Ravensberg on his side of the line—hardly a trio of heavyweights, but they had plenty of experience, intelligence and quickness.

Ciolli started the next week against Northwestern, but he knew at game time that, from that point on, he had competition from returning war veteran Howard Brown. At 5-11, 200 pounds, Brown was quick and agile and had been a starter on McMillin's highly regarded 1942 squad. The Northwestern game was still in the first half when Brown replaced Ciolli. Brown's widow, Dixie, recalled fifty years later: "Howard comes out of service and bumps Frank Ciolli out of the line immediately. Howard felt bad about this because Frank had been playing, and yet he and Frank remained the best of friends." Ciolli didn't start again in '45, but saw enough action to become an essential part of this championship team. He remembers the tie at Northwestern as a pivotal game, coming on the heels of the Hoosiers' upset of Michigan. "I think Northwestern kind of woke us up," Ciolli said. "We lost our overconfidence, but still we knew we were going to win those ball games."

Like all of his teammates, Ciolli has vivid memories of the the intense cold at Minnesota and the cold rain the next week at Pittsburgh. "At the start of the [Minnesota] game, they cleared the field off, and you could see the steam coming up. So, within four or five minutes, you can imagine stepping in mud which would freeze every time you fell down." Even though he played another year at Bloomington, Ciolli cites the 1945 Purdue game as the highlight of his IU experience. "We were really ready," he recalls. "It was a hard-fought game, but we knew that we were going to come out of it, and we did. The emotion was so high it was hard to explain."

After graduation, Ciolli married Betty West from Bloomington. Now living in Terre Haute, they have four children, a girl and three boys. Frank ended up doing something he always wanted to do—coaching, retiring in 1990. Now he works part-time at the *Terre Haute Tribune*.

He still follows the Hoosiers on television, both basketball and football. "I just love football," he says with no trace of regret. "I played it ever since elementary school in Ohio. I never thought of size and all. I got the hell beat out of me, but I think I got my licks in too."

How would Frank Ciolli like to be remembered? "Just as one of the players who was tickled pink to be on the 1945 squad." When asked to name outstanding players on the 1945 team, though, he demurs. "You couldn't pick out any outstanding player. I think they were all about equal. Pihos and Taliaferro were a little better, but you know the line had a lot to do with it."

As a member of that line and that team, whether on the sidelines or in the game, nobody gave more than Frank Ciolli.

−17−

DICK DERANEK

On November 22, 1947, as Dick Deranek walked off the field at Indiana's Memorial Stadium for the last time, he did so with a sense of accomplishment. He had played four years at Indiana University and had never lost to Purdue. Even more significant, with Deranek on the Indiana squad, the team had won or tied twenty-seven of thirty-eight games beginning in 1944. And Deranek did his part in establishing that record. In Indiana's championship season of 1945, he rushed twenty-one times for 248 yards, an amazing average of 11.8 yards per carry. In the crucial Michigan victory that year, despite suffering a shoulder injury earlier in practice, he ran three times for fifty-three yards. Not only could he run, he caught passes and returned punts for touchdowns. In 1945, he caught five passes for 123 yards, an average of 24.6 yards per reception. With time running out and Indiana clinging to a 7–2 lead over powerful Tulsa, they gave the ball to Dick Deranek. He could do it all.

In high school in the early 1940s, Deranek was a prep phenom at South Bend Central High School. In 1942, his junior year, he scored eight touchdowns. As team captain the following year, he did even better, scoring eleven touchdowns in a variety of ways: running, catching passes, returning punts. He even tossed a touchdown pass to his brother.

Even in wartime 1944, Deranek was sought after by all of the major colleges, including Notre Dame, Purdue, Nebraska, and Illinois. Deranek, who had received a 4-F deferment, initially selected Purdue, but that was before he'd met Alvin Nugent McMillin. Dick's high school coaches, Indiana grad Jim Crowe and former Indiana All-American Corby Davis, suggested he visit Bo in Bloomington. Deranek did and committed to attend Indiana before he left campus, joining a select group of freshmen who formed the foundation for the four most successful years in Indiana football history.

Under wartime rules, freshmen were permitted to participate with the varsity in 1944. Deranek took advantage of the opportunity by becoming a sixty-minute performer. He played right end, left end, left halfback, and right halfback. By midseason he was starting at right halfback. And he left no doubts that his high school talents would easily transfer to collegiate play. In Indiana's 1944 early season upset of Michigan, Deranek intercepted a pass. In the opening game, he scored a touchdown against Fort Knox, later intercepted a Northwestern pass and then scored twice against Iowa. Against Ohio State at Columbus, he caught a TD pass in Indiana's heartbreaking loss to the champion Buckeyes. Finally, against Pittsburgh, he scored twice, once on a run and again on a pass reception. Indiana was called the best civilian team in the country in 1944, and eighteen-year-old Dick Deranek tied for the team lead in scoring. No wonder he and McMillin both looked forward to his return in 1945.

The world turned around several times in 1945. The war ended, the atomic age was born and suddenly the United States had a new adversary in the Soviet Union. For Deranek, the year tested his resolve; despite his great freshman season, he found himself sharing right halfback duties with Mel Groomes, a 6-foot, 170-pound sophomore from Trenton, New Jersey. Groomes had originally been slated for left halfback, but the emergence of freshman George Taliaferro allowed McMillin to move Groomes to right halfback. Groomes had played little in 1944, but his quickness caught McMillin's attention in 1945. And so Deranek and Groomes shared the right halfback position offensively, with Groomes also playing defense. Groomes recalled: "Dick and I played the same position, but when I was in the game and we would get down to around the five-yard line, Dick would enter the game and run an end-around. His speed was just right to run that play."

Despite reduced playing time, Deranek's 1945 statistics were outstanding. But No. 88 gave much of the credit to his teammates, and to McMillin in particular. "In 1945, we first used the 4–4 defense and it completely baffled the opposition," Deranek recalled. "This is the first time anyone had used the defense, and the other teams had no idea what was going on. Their blocking was way off." For all his innovative brilliance, though, McMillin could occasionally get confused. Deranek remembers the practice session in which Bo was ecstatic, thinking he'd devised a perfect play. Then someone on defense yelled: "Bo, we've got twelve men on the field." McMillin would also sometimes yell for a player to go into the game, only to find out the lad was already on the field.

"Bo was a very intense coach, but he was loyal to you," Deranek recalled. "He would do anything for you. I respected him, and I thought that he was a great guy." One personal incident demonstrates the reason for Deranek's fondness for his coach. Before the Minnesota game, the weather was cool in Bloomington—and even colder in Minneapolis. "So I went into Bo's office and told him, 'Bo, I'm going to freeze up there. I don't even own a topcoat.' He said, 'Well you go downtown to Kahn's clothing store and pick out a coat or whatever you want and put it on my account.'"

Throughout Deranek's last two years with the Hoosiers, he showed versatility and talent despite the competition from returning servicemen. "We had so many good ballplayers in 1946, and Bo tried to get everybody in," Deranek recalled. "As a result, we had no continuity initially. We got straightened out, but at one time we had three or four guys playing right halfback, all of whom had started at one time or another in the past."

Still, Deranek's career statistics show 158 carries for 1,036 yards, an impressive 7.2 yards per carry. Obviously, Dick Deranek was headed for professional football. But first he participated in the annual North-South post-season game in 1947, where, not surprisingly, the writers voted him the North's outstanding back.

The day of the North-South game, Deranek began negotiating separately with Baltimore coach Cecil Isbell and Jock Sutherland of the Pittsburgh Steelers. McMillin, one of the North coaches, sat in the lobby of the Baltimore Hotel to advise Dick on which offer to accept. Dick and Bo settled on a no-cut contract with Pittsburgh at $650 a game, plus a $1,000 signing bonus.

Regrettably, Deranek's professional career was over almost before it began. An ankle injury suffered in practice was severe enough that Pittsburgh had no choice but to release him. But he got his money and, a bit later, an invitation from McMillin to join Bo with the Detroit Lions. But Deranek's football career was over at this juncture, and he decided to get married and pursue a business career. After short stints selling sporting goods and automobile tires, he went into the finance business, where he found his niche with the Teachers Credit Union, becoming a vice-president before his retirement. Deranek and his wife have three sons, one of whom played high school football.

Reflecting on the 1945 team's success, he said, "What did it? Unity. We pulled for each other, whether in or out of the ball game. As soon as someone came out of the game, we would question the player as to what was going on. Everybody just believed in everyone else, and we had confidence."

It was easy to have confidence in Dick Deranek. As George Taliaferro recalls: "Dick was a guy who was supremely confident as to what he could do and couldn't do. He prepared himself to the best of his abilities. A quiet guy who apparently knew his lot was not on the main stage, but decided he would be the best he could be—and he was."

-18-
MEL GROOMES

In 1944 Trenton, New Jersey, was, like all American cities, a town that had gone to war. Avenger planes were being built at Eastern Aircraft there, and General Electric had a Fisher Guide plant in Trenton. (It's still there.) At Trenton High School, the largest in New Jersey, four thousand students prepared for the future under less-than-promising circumstances. One, a slender, six-foot-tall black kid named Mel Groomes, was making his mark in athletics. Slightly built but exceptionally fast, he won all-state honors in football, basketball and track and was the first black to play American Legion baseball with a white team.

Despite his athletic accomplishments, few colleges showed interest in Groomes during the summer of 1944 because of his color. Major league baseball was three years away from Jackie Robinson's debut. Basketball coaches in the Big Ten Athletic Conference followed an unwritten rule excluding blacks, and black football players were seldom welcome outside schools in a limited area of the Midwest and East. It was no surprise then, that young Mel Groomes ended up applying to one of these Eastern schools, Temple University in Philadelphia. But after three weeks on campus, during which he practiced with the Temple football team, Groomes was told that he couldn't enroll because he'd failed the entrance exam. Temple coach Ray Morrison suggested that Groomes consider Indiana University. Morrison called his friend, Hoosier coach Bo McMillin, and Bo welcomed the new recruit.

So in September 1944, the young athlete packed what clothes he had, accepted ten dollars from his sister, and took the train to Indianapolis, later boarding a bus for Bloomington. Mrs. McMillin met him at the bus station and immediately drove him to the football stadium, where he met Bo and a few of the players. "Bo told me he would get me in the school the next morning," Groomes recalled. "He got me a uniform and a place to live; and on Tuesday, just two days after leaving Philadelphia, I practiced with the team," Groomes recalled. That Saturday he played for the Hoosiers, mostly on defense.

Groomes would later learn that fate—and Southern racism—were instrumental in his transfer to Indiana. Temple officials, discovering the school's 1944 football schedule included several Southern colleges which had refused to compete against "negroes," opted to tell Groomes that he had failed the academic exam when, in fact, he had passed.

A year later, after the Hoosiers had won the championship and McMillin was named coach of the year, Temple's coach called to congratulate Bo. McMillin thanked Morrison, then asked his Philadelphia friend if he had any more players over there like Mel Groomes. "If you do, I'll be glad to take them," Bo quipped.

Groomes' contributions to Indiana football fortunes were minimal in 1944. A defensive specialist at that time, he played just enough to gain the experience necessary to compete in 1945. And compete he did—on offense and defense—contributing mightily to the Hoosiers' unbeaten record. In the championship year, Groomes rushed 51 times for 249 yards, an outstanding average of 4.9 yards per carry. He also caught 12 passes for 223 yards and completed two of four passes himself. Not bad for a defensive specialist.

Despite his accomplishments, he retained a refreshing humility. "I came from a great high school program; I didn't think I was a star or someone great," Groomes said. Besides, he added, "the individual Indiana players were so great themselves that there wasn't any room for someone to think: 'I'm the reason the team did so well.'"

Groomes fondly recalls all of his teammates, particularly Howard Brown. "Howard was the greatest. He made us welcome, put his arm around our shoulders and told us, 'don't worry.'" One incident in particular illustrated Brown's protective nature. Groomes recalled the 1945 Purdue game, in which a Boilermaker lineman had roughed up Groomes after Mel had carried the ball. Returning to the huddle, Groomes mentioned the incident to his teammates. Brown immediately turned to quarterback Ben Raimondi and said the Hoosiers shouldn't allow any player to be treated that way, regardless of his color. And so Indiana began running plays at—and through—this Purdue lineman, over Deal and Sowinski. "They just hammered him and straightened him up," Groomes recalled. "Purdue was the dirtiest team we played that year as far as I was concerned," he added. "I was safer on the field though, because when I would be tackled out of bounds on the Purdue sideline, all of their players would kick me in the back and head. As soon as I could, I'd get up and run back on the field."

After graduation from IU in 1947, Groomes followed McMillin to Detroit, where be became the first black to play for the Lions. Two years later, he earned his master's degree at Rutgers University and, in April 1951, he married. In July of that year, he joined the Air Force. During his four-year tour of duty, he coached and played with the Bolling Air Force Base team, the National Service Champions in 1952 and '53. "I had a wonderful time in the Air Force," Groomes recalled. "I coached two years at Howard University in Washington near Bolling and ended up at North Carolina A&T in 1955." He stayed there for two decades, winning several championships.

"I coached football for twenty years, baseball for thirty-one and taught for thirty-four, Groomes said, "then I lost my eyesight and retired." As a former coach himself, Groomes is quick to credit Bo McMillin for his innovative style, especially his 4–4 defense. "I mean, they talk about the 4–4 today, and I'm telling people: 'Hell, I played that back in 1945.' All they do today is borrow what was done then and add a few wrinkles to it."

Groomes is rightfully proud of his accomplishments. "Being on that first Big Ten championship team with a wonderful group of players . . . and having only one pass completed against me in four years, that was great." But Groomes' pride can't match his admirable humility. When asked how he'd like to be remembered, he replied: "Well, I'd like for them to say: 'He was a nice fellow who played his role, wasn't a loudmouth and was a nice person to know—a guy who graduated in four years.' "

In October 1995, Groomes returned to Bloomington for the team's fifty-year reunion. Though blind and in a wheelchair because of diabetes, his mind was clear, his speech distinct and his memory excellent. At that reunion, his teammates recalled what was perhaps Groomes' greatest performance—against Purdue in 1945. He had several long runs on offense, and he helped the Hoosier defense hold Purdue scoreless. No one present at that game will ever forget the Purdue passes he deflected at the last instant. And in the third quarter, with the game still scoreless, his twenty-five-yard sprint behind Cannady, Deal, and Sowinski led to Indiana's first score.

George Taliaferro remembers his teammate as an incredible athlete: "At six feet tall and 171 pounds, he was the hardest hitter on the team," Taliaferro marveled. "And he could run like a streak," John Cannady added. "Mel was just a real good kid."

A good kid and a great defensive back—the best ever to play at Indiana University.

–19–
JOE SOWINSKI

During the thirties and forties college football featured sixty-minute players—"iron man" competitors who refused to leave the game. This was the era of two-way players; specialists were generally limited to kickoffs and defensive play, and the rules effectively discouraged substitution. Indiana fit in with this trend. Hoosier end coach Johnny Kovatch routinely told his linemen: "Be prepared to go sixty." And from 1943 through 1945, none of Kovatch's crew went the distance more often than tackle and guard Joe Sowinski.

Entering Indiana as an nineteen-year-old freshman in September 1943, it took just a few games before Joe Sowinski was in Bo McMillin's starting lineup—and he stayed. During the 1944 season, Sowinski was on the field an astounding 524 minutes out of a possible 600. By 1945, Joe was a fixture at guard, having moved from tackle. At 6 feet, 200 pounds, the quiet kid from East Chicago was a mainstay in the Hoosiers' championship lineup. Sophomore Bob Harbison from Evansville replaced Sowinski from time to time, but he knew his place. "I wasn't a very good football player," he said modestly, "but I was surrounded by a lot of good football players—including Joe Sowinski."

It was Pete Rucinski, coach at East Chicago Roosevelt High School, who had recommended Sowinski to Hoosier scout and recruiting ace Paul "Pooch" Harrell. Even though Sowinski had skipped his senior year because of osteomyelitis in his left leg, he accepted an Indiana scholarship. An Indianapolis doctor had examined the leg and said the infection wouldn't worsen. Still, for four years, Joe was forced to wear a plastic shin guard whenever he played or practiced.

Shortly after his arrival—and for four years after—Joe Sowinski was inseparable from Indiana University and Bo

McMillin. A high school wrestling champion, Sowinksi visited Indiana as a participant in a state high school tourney at the Indiana fieldhouse. "When I had a chance to play football at Indiana, I was really excited about it," he recalled. He also was excited about his coach. "When I came down (to Bloomington) to meet Bo, I was really impressed. He had spoken at my high school and was quite a gentleman, as well as a speaker. He was a great man."

After serving his apprenticeship in the line during the 1943 and 1944 seasons, Sowinski had the experience that enabled him to make major contributions in 1945. "We had a real good nucleus for a ball club," he recalled of the '45 squad. "I remember Bo writing us that summer and telling us that the older ballplayers would be about two weeks late reporting because he felt the freshmen needed more work, although he was very impressed by the first-year players."

In 1945 the iron man started every game, though he did get some relief that season as the Hoosiers blitzed Nebraska, Iowa and Cornell College. By Purdue weekend, Joe was ready—even anxious—to go sixty minutes. "I think the team as a whole felt apprehensive, but still confident; we felt we could beat Purdue. We knew what the game meant."

After clinching the title in that game, the locker room scene was unforgettable, Sowinski recalled. "Bo's old team from Centre College was present, and many of them spoke to us as a team. It was very impressive." The players' fondness for McMillin even made them back down a bit from their plan to throw their mentor into the shower. "We kind of looked at Bo, and we said we didn't want to hurt him. But, since he didn't give much resistance, we slowly put him under the shower."

Even today, Sowinski's admiration for McMillin is boundless. "Bo was a very creative person—very inspirational. He came up with a new offense, the cockeyed-T, a combination of single-wing and T-formation. . . . It gave us a little advantage offensively. Defensively, Bo was the first coach in the country to come out with the 4–4–3 defense. It was very imaginative."

In 1947, Joe Sowinski concluded his Indiana career, graduating with a degree in education. He was drafted by the New York Giants and considered playing professional football. But, having survived four years of college line play with his bad leg, he opted not to pursue the pro game. Instead, teaching and coaching became his vocation. He spent thirty-eight years in high schools, twenty coaching both football and wrestling, seventeen coaching wrestling alone, and one final year without sports. Married in 1947, Sowinski and his wife have two grown children, a son and a daughter. And, true to his iron man reputation, his health is good.

When asked to compare today's players with those of his time, Sowinski has some clear opinions. "Although it's hard to judge teams from different eras, I don't believe the guys today are as skilled or well-rounded as we were at that time," he says. "The ballplayers then had to play both offensively and defensively. We had to master more skills."

According to his teammates, few mastered those skills better or applied them more consistently than big Joe Sowinski. "Joe was nice, just a great big teddy bear, but he was a tough football player," Tom Schwartz recalled. "You try to block him and you had your hands full. He's just a nice guy who was a fine football player."

Despite his serious leg condition and the fact that he could see little beyond the line of scrimmage without his eyeglasses, Sowinski started every Hoosier game for three and one-half years. He was an important component in Indiana's 1945 championship.

And how does Sowinski himself want to be remembered? "Just as Bo indicated in an article he once wrote: 'Sowinski was one of the most dependable ballplayers I ever coached. You could count on him every Saturday.'"

–20–
RUSSELL "MUTT" DEAL

In the late summer of 1940, with Great Britain suffering horrendous losses from German air raids and Japan continuing its aggression against China, the American people remained divided over participation in the war. Little did they know that this would be their last year of peace for four long years.

Far away from the world stage, in the small town of Bicknell, Indiana (population 5,110), eighteen-year-old Russell "Mutt" Deal was preparing for his first year of college. An all-state football player at Bicknell High School, Deal had chosen Indiana University to continue his education, having been offered a football scholarship.

Although the 1940 enrollment at Indiana was nowhere near the record set after World War II, it still was a big step for a kid from a small southwest Indiana coal-mining town. But "Mutt," as he had been nicknamed at age five, was a strong-willed young man. He first met Bo McMillin as a result of contacts by Bicknell Indiana Boosters. Bo liked what he saw, despite the fact that Deal was blind in his left eye. "It doesn't make any difference," said Bo. "We'd like to have you come to Indiana University."

The players McMillin had recruited for his 1940 freshman squad were exceptional, perhaps the greatest freshman group ever assembled at Indiana. In Billy Hillenbrand of Evansville and Lou Saban of LaGrange, Illinois, Bo had a couple of athletes who had been heavily recruited by the "big boys."

The next year, despite the presence of his talented sophomores on the 1941 varsity, the Hoosiers disappointed their followers by winning only two games. But Deal got in his first game, playing backup guard in Indiana's opening loss to Notre Dame at South Bend. "Definitely a thrill," he recalled.

In 1942, Deal made the starting lineup—all 195 pounds of

him. He played left tackle, joining a couple of talented sophomores on the line: Howard Brown at right guard and Pete Pihos
at right end. With a 7–3 record, the '42 squad was one of Bo's
best, but losses to Iowa and Ohio State denied them the conference title.

Russ Deal lasted at Indiana until August 1943, but on his
third visit to the draft board, he was inducted—despite the loss
of one eye. Two years later, in August 1945, while serving in an
injury-reconditioning program at Louisville, Kentucky, he was
discharged because of a lifelong problem with migraine head-
aches. "I'd had no correspondence with Bo, so I sent him a letter
saying I was about to be discharged," Deal recalled. "I drove to
Bloomington and Bo said: 'Get dressed, you can practice immediately.' But I was married then, so I told him: 'I'll be back September first, and I will be in shape!' "

And so, having played no football since November 1942, Mutt
Deal joined the squad in preparing for its opening game with
Michigan. School didn't start until after the Michigan game, but
Mutt still kept football in perspective. "I was more mature and
responsible," he remembered, "The Army taught me that studies
came first."

After upsetting the Wolverines, Deal and his teammates welcomed Brown and Pihos back, but still almost lost that week at
Northwestern. Deal recalled: "We kidded them, saying: 'If you
two guys had stayed at home, we would've won the ball game!' "
Still, the soon-to-be-champion Hoosiers had begun to coalesce,
and one of their first steps toward success was to name Deal
acting captain.

By the time the Hoosiers disposed of Illinois with a new play
devised by McMillin which involved Kluszewski as a passer, Deal
felt the team was really coming together thanks to the sixty-
minute play of Sowinski, himself and others. Deal recalled assistant coach John Kovatch saying, "You've got to go for sixty. If you
get hurt, you'll have to play anyway." Captain Deal set a good
example. "I didn't want to be taken out unless I was really hurt,"
he said.

Because of his experience, skill and durability, Deal called
plays on defense. "I always worked with Bo," he recalled. "We
would get together and see what defense we would play." This
was the year of Bo's 4–4 defense—signified by Deal's "thumbs-
up" signal to his teammates. When he wanted a six-man line,

Deal would signal "thumbs down," with variations if opponents put a flanker on Deal's side of the line.

Following the Illinois game, the Hoosiers were tested only once—by Tulsa. Games against Nebraska, Iowa, Cornell College and Minnesota permitted the regulars much-needed rest. By the time they visited Pittsburgh on November 17, the team began to relax somewhat, saving their best for Purdue the following Saturday.

By the week of the Purdue game, tension was growing considerably, the campus was all but deserted because of Thanksgiving vacation, practices were arduous, and Bo became more worrisome and superstitious. Deal recalled one morning that week: he and Howard Brown were having breakfast at a campus hangout called the Gables when an agitated McMillin came in and sat in their booth. "Them stinking newspaper people," he fumed. Apparently the morning edition of *The Indianapolis Star* had an article on Pete Pihos, saying his return from the service had saved the season for Indiana. "They'll destroy everything we have worked for," Bo complained. Deal and Brown assured Bo that they knew how to handle Pihos and the team. And they did.

On Thursday, Thanksgiving Day, the team held practice and then adjourned to the Union Building for their holiday dinner. This time, Deal recalled, Bo casually pulled a chair up to the table where Deal and Pihos were eating. "Boys," he said, "I know your wives are coming in tonight, and you know how important this game is to us." The "boys" responded: "Yes sir, Bo." He said, "Well, I'm going to ask you not to have any family relations tonight." Deal wouldn't say whether he and Pihos heeded Bo's advice, but two days later they earned their first conference championship with a 26–0 win over the Boilermakers.

After graduation in June 1946, Deal began a long career at Hobart High School in northwest Indiana. He was head football coach for eighteen years and principal for thirteen years. Two of his sons, Mike and Mark, played football at Indiana, and Mark was recently named an assistant coach of the Hoosiers under Bill Mallory.

Fifty years after the championship season, Mutt's teammates recalled their captain with admiration. "Deal was a fighter," Joe Sowinski said. "If he missed a block, you could be sure his feet would kick you one way or another."

George Taliaferro remembered Deal's uncanny ability to sense pressure from an opponent. "He didn't have to see you on his blind side, he felt you," Taliaferro said. "And then he turned on you like a rattlesnake."

"Mutt was a leader," Charlie Armstrong added, "tough and aggressive."

At the end of the 1945 season, the team rewarded Deal's leadership by voting him "permanent" captain. And in 1993, he was voted into the Indiana University Athletic Hall of Fame. When asked how he'd like to be remembered by Indiana fans, Deal had little use for words. He simply held up his Hall of Fame ring.

–21–

JOHN CANNADY

John Hanley Cannady came to Bloomington in the late summer of 1943 by way of South Carolina and Kentucky. Cannady, a three-year prep player at Spartansburg, South Carolina, and an all-state and all-Southern player at Owensboro (Kentucky) High School his senior year, was one of Bo McMillin's best finds in his fourteen years at Indiana.

Cannady's father died when John was sixteen, and the budding athlete spent his last year of high school living with an aunt in Owensboro. Although he was apparently headed for the University of Kentucky, Cannady's running exploits during his senior season attracted Alvin McMillin, thanks to a tip from a friendly Owensboro physician. It didn't take long for Bo to convince Cannady that his future rested among the stone quarries and rolling hills of southern Indiana. Cannady liked Bo immediately. "A great man," he recalled in a South Carolina drawl still noticeable five decades after his playing days. "He was just like a daddy to me, and his wife and children and all of them. I was just a country boy, and they taught me just like my mother and dad. I thought I was in the Hall of Fame there."

Cannady quickly established his presence in the Hoosiers' plans for 1943. Listed as a quarterback (blocking back) in McMillin's single-wing formation, he showed his versatility by occasionally moving to right guard. Indiana football programs of 1943 listed Cannady at 5-11, 190 pounds. He would get bigger as his Indiana career flourished. As a letterman in 1944, Cannady again played in both the line and backfield, but was then listed at 6-1 and 195. He had been good enough in '43 to have been chosen along with Bob Ravensberg and Pete Pihos to play in the College All-Star Game in Chicago that summer of 1944. Though reports of his size varied widely, all who saw him agreed that he was an impressive specimen. "John Cannady had the biggest calves of any person symmetrically I have ever seen," recalled George Taliaferro. Reserve tackle Bob Joseph noted with awe: "He weighed about 240 pounds—with no fat on him."

By the summer of 1945, now listed at 6-1, 210 pounds, Cannady was scheduled to be the Hoosiers' starting fullback. But he never lined up in back of the center again. While practicing that summer, he injured his knee and was unable to make Indiana's season-opening trip to Ann Arbor. Nick Lysohir, a 5-foot-10, 170-pound freshman from Sharon, Pennsylvania, started in his place. It was the only game Cannady would miss in his four years. And it was a game that caused problems for Bo McMillin. Before halftime in that upset win over Michigan, center Bob Meyer had broken his leg. Postgame examinations ruled him out for the rest of the season. McMillin was in a quandary and publicly acknowledged that center and fullback were concerns. But, just as in the movies of that era, a happy ending was forthcoming. Pete Pihos reported to the squad and was moved to fullback. Cannady, his knee healed, moved back to the line, taking Meyer's spot at center. Bo now had his team. By using Pihos and Cannady to back up the Hoosier line, McMillin had what halfback Dick Deranek would later call "two of the greatest linebackers I have ever seen." In 1945, most coaches in the country shared that assessment.

Although he received no post-season honors in 1945, Cannady was selected to the All Big Ten team in 1946 and was named a second-team All-American. And in August of 1947, he, along with teammates Deal and Raimondi, participated in the College All-Star game in Chicago and helped Coach Frank Leahy of Notre Dame beat the Champion Chicago Bears 16–0. Cannady didn't just play, he was good enough to start at center for the All-Stars. Cannady recalls the prominence of Army players on that team: "Davis and Blanchard never said much, but there were four or five of them in the line that said to the rest of us: 'Well, you boys can just lay back now. The big Army's here.' I remember every time we scrimmaged the sons of bitches, we'd blow them out."

When John Cannady began his long professional career with the New York Giants, he left an impressive trail of off-field exploits in Bloomington. Several of his teammates and others recalled the legend of "Bubba" Cannady, a free spirit who was clearly less than enthusiastic about the academic aspects of college life. His linebacker partner, Pete Pihos, remembers Cannady as "not the greatest student in the world." Dick Deranek recalled John as "happy go lucky." After the Purdue game he disappeared and we didn't see him for a month or two." (When asked fifty years later, Cannady replied, "They weren't looking for me.") Center Bob Meyer remembers Cannady most for his persistent sleep-walking habit. "One night he walked right out of a window at the Alpha Tau Omega fraternity house," Meyer recalled. "Luckily, he didn't fall too far."

John Cannady himself admits he was a loner. "I ran around with a little guy named Joe Roman. He's dead now. He was a wrestler, and I believe his son still runs the family pub in Bloomington." John also worked for the owners of Nick's, a popular tavern in Bloomington. At that time Cannady was living year round in Bloomington, and he had to work to eat. He said he did it "anyway I could," and that included being a bouncer.

But for all his raucous behavior, Cannady was well-liked by those whose lives he touched. Mel Groomes remembers a serious fellow on the field "but just a wonderful person." Howard Brown's widow, Dixie, remembers inviting John to dinner. "He was very, very nice—a good ol' boy."

If there were any doubts about Cannady's ability to play professional football, his career with the New York Giants dispelled them summarily. New York's number two draft pick in 1947, he received a three-year, no-cut contract and a four-thousand-dollar signing bonus. The Giants never regretted their decision. John played eight years in New York as a blocking back and linebacker, and was named to the All-Pro teams of 1950 and 1952. Unfortunately, the Giants never won a championship during his tenure, but John has always had an answer: "In 1950 we had the best defense in the league. But God damn, we never could get any offense. They wouldn't pay anybody any money."

Following his retirement from football, Cannady returned to Charleston, where he initially helped out friends by working in a local bar at twelve dollars a night.

But he soon he opened his own establishment called John's Bar, and it became a fixture in historic Charleston for the thirty-eight years Cannady owned it. He recently sold his interest to third parties, who wisely retained the name and his memorabilia.

More than fifty years have passed since John Hanley Cannady arrived in Bloomington. Poor health now prevents him from returning to campus; his last visit was twenty-six years ago. But the image of Big John has survived among his contemporaries, as have the memories of his on-field prowess. Larry Napolitan, Pete Pihos, and Wally Getz all remember John as "one hell of a football player." Longtime Indianapolis broadcaster Tom Carnegie recalled Cannady as "just a rock, unbelievably strong." Frank Ciolli described him succinctly: "He was tough. He took no prisoners." And assistant coach Pooch Harrell, who watched John throughout his four years at IU, once said of Cannady: "I've never seen anybody that could shoot the gap (blitz) and throw a guy for a loss and then on the next play intercept a pass ten or fifteen yards downfield." Since Harrell made that statement, John Cannady has acquired some company in that elite class, men named Dick Butkus, Ray Nitschke, and Jack Lambert, among others. Pretty good company for a South Carolina country boy.

–22–
PETE PIHOS

In late November of 1945, Bo McMillin called Pete Pihos the greatest football player in Western Conference (Big Ten) history. Fifty years later George Taliaferro referred to him as "without question, the greatest football player ever to attend Indiana University." Pihos is the only Indiana player to be named an All-American at two positions, end and fullback. He's the only Indiana player in the Pro Football Hall of Fame, and one of only a few IU players in the College Football Hall of Fame. He was one of the last NFL players to compete on both offense and defense and was an NFL All-Pro six times: five times on offense, once on defense. Unquestionably, Pete Pihos is an Indiana football legend.

The legend began in Chicago, where Pihos' family moved from Orlando, Florida, before World War II. Pete enrolled at Austin High School, then one of Chicago's great prep football programs. In 1937, Austin had competed for the city championship in front of 125,000 fans in Chicago's Soldier Field. It was the right place at the right time for young Pihos. Despite the residue of a south Florida drawl, he was readily accepted and starred for Austin in his last two years of high school. In his senior year, scholarship opportunities abounded—Northwestern and Michigan, among others. But in the late spring of 1941, Pihos fell under the spell of the charismatic McMillin. After hearing Bo speak, "I just thought he was the greatest guy in the world," Pihos recalled. "That's why I decided to go to Indiana University. I had an academic scholarship because I made all A's at Austin," he added, "I was just tickled to be there, a beautiful campus. And Bo became like a father to me since my own father was murdered when I was eleven years old."

The freshman team assembled at Indiana that fall included not only Pihos, but the players who would form the nucleus of Bo's fine 1942 team: Lou Gambino, Jimmy Dewar, Hugh

McKinnis, Bob Cowan, Paul Walker, and others. Pihos settled in at right end in 1942, and Indiana lost only three games. He led the Hoosiers with twenty-one pass receptions for 295 yards, a fourteen-yard average. It was enough to earn him a spot among the College All- Stars in the summer of 1943 for their traditional game against the professional Washington Redskins. Pete had a wonderful time as he and legendary quarterback Otto Graham helped the All-Stars win 27-7.

In 1943, Pihos earned his first All-America designation, although the military draft had decimated the team that year. Of the thirty-nine squad members that September, thirty-four were freshmen. Yet, despite the inability to use Army and Navy trainees on campus (including Billy Hillenbrand and Lou Saban), McMillin managed to win four games and tie two. And three of his four losses were to top-ten teams—Michigan, Purdue, and Great Lakes. One of the thirty-four freshmen that year, an eighteen-year-old kid out of Cincinnati named Bob "Hunchy" Hoernsmeyer, established himself as one of the nation's top backs, breaking Michigan star Tom Harmon's conference record for total offense. Pihos did his part too, catching a team-high nineteen passes for 262 yards. And when the Hoosiers shut out Wisconsin 34–0 on October 23, Pihos tied an Indiana record with three touchdowns in one game.

After playing in the East-West game in San Francisco on New Year's Day 1944, Pihos traded in his football uniform for one of Army khaki. "I volunteered for the infantry, and I must have been crazy," he recalled. "I was in the Thirty-fifth Infantry Division, and we hit the beaches in Europe thirty days after D-Day. Before it was over, I had four battle stars and a battlefield commission." After Germany's surrender, Pihos' division was scheduled to be part of a massive force assembled to invade Japan. Fortunately, the Japanese surrendered in August 1945, after atomic bombs had devastated Hiroshima and Nagasaki.

Before the end of September, Pihos decided to return to Indiana. Though still officially in the Army, he had accumulated ninety days' leave. Sometime during the weekend of the Michigan game on September 22, he and Howard Brown, also on leave, crossed paths at the Indianapolis Athletic Club with—who else?— Bo McMillin. They discussed arrangements for the boys' return to campus. On September 24, when Bo was a guest of honor at the Indianapolis Downtown Quarterback Club luncheon, Pihos and Brown, both still in uniform, shared the dais with him. In his speech that day, Bo hinted at their return, but more or less alluded to the 1946 season. Bo could always keep a straight face when he had to, and this was one of those times. Pihos and Brown were enrolled and practicing for Northwestern by midweek.

With only three practices under his belt, Pihos didn't start the Northwestern game. But when Northwestern scored early, he and Brown came off the bench in a hurry. They never returned to it. It was Pete's touchdown (and the extra point by kicker Charlie Armstrong) that enabled Indiana to tie the Wildcats that day. "I thought at the time there wasn't anybody else who could have made that touchdown but Pete," Armstrong recalled later. "He had several people on his back."

The remainder of the 1945 season was a tour de force for Pihos and the Hoosiers. One incident near the end of the first half in the Minnesota game illustrates the Hoosiers' commitment to Bo's charge: "Have confidence, believe in yourself." "I was calling the plays and we were down on the Minnesota two-yard line," Pihos remembers. "I called my own play but didn't make it. Now it's third down with no time for a huddle, so I called the play out loud: 'Same play—on three,' and we scored that touchdown before halftime."

By season's end, Pihos had rushed for 410 yards on ninety-two carries (including 113 yards in the mud at Pittsburgh), caught five passes, completed the only pass he threw, and scored eight touchdowns. He was named to the All Big Ten squad and was accorded second-team All-America honors by *Liberty* magazine, United Press, the *Sporting News*, and the American Football Coaches Association.

Following the Purdue game, Pete reported back to the service, only to find the Army wanted to discharge him so that he could play for the Hoosiers in a proposed post-season charity game against Army. Pihos balked, telling the general, "I don't want anything I don't deserve. All I want to know is when I'll get out. So he said, 'You'll be in school in January,' and I said 'OK, that's the way it's going to be.'"

Two events in 1945 and '46 greatly affected Pihos' future. First, he was drafted by the Philadelphia Eagles; second, he enrolled in law school at Indiana University. Pihos never got his law degree, but he hit the jackpot with his career as a professional football player. Joining the Eagles for the 1947 season after helping the Hoosiers to a winning season in 1946, Pete moved back to end, his preferred position, and helped the Eagles to three straight division championships and two NFL titles. In 1947 the Chicago Cardinals stopped the Eagles 28–21; but in 1948 and 1949, Philadelphia overcame rain, snow, the Cardinals and the Los Angeles Rams for consecutive titles. Pihos' postseason share was $754 in 1947, about $1,300 in 1948, and $1,096 in 1949. The Eagles won no more championships during Pihos' tenure through 1955, and they lost their coach, Earl "Greasy" Neal, after a losing 1950 season. Neal was replaced by Bo McMillin in 1951, one year before the Colonel's death.

Pete Pihos contributed significantly to professional football and the Philadelphia Eagles. United Press named him an end on its NFL team in 1948, as both Associated Press and United Press did the following year. In 1949, he caught the winning touchdown pass in the NFL championship game. He played in the first six Pro Bowl games and finished his professional career with consecutive All-Pro selections from 1952 through 1955. Beginning in 1953, he led the league in pass receptions three straight years, sharing the title with Billy Wilson of the San Francisco Forty-Niners in 1954. He finished his career with 373 catches for 5,619 yards and 378 points.

The January 1955 issue of *Sport*, then the country's premier sports magazine, featured Pihos on its cover with a companion story titled "The Old Pro." In all caps, *Sport* sang Pete's praises: "a hard worker and a loquacious teammate, Pihos is an excellent offensive blocker and top pass catcher. Not especially fast, Pete fakes well, has good moves in the secondary, always seems to know what he is doing, and has remarkable hands." The "old pro" was thirty years old.

In 1970, Pete earned the highest honor a football player can receive when he was inducted into the professional football Hall of Fame in Canton, Ohio. His friend Howard Brown introduced him. That year, the twenty-fifth anniversary of the Hoosiers' Big Ten championship, also marked Pihos' most recent visit to Indiana University.

Pihos had married a Philadelphia woman, with whom he had four children, two boys and two girls. Tragically, his wife died when the youngest child, a daughter, was only six months old. Eight years later, while working for an insurance company in Fort Wayne, he married again, this time to a woman he'd met in

Greensboro, North Carolina. That marriage ended in divorce. Pete is seventy-two now and retired from the insurance business, spending his time traveling throughout the country, often playing in charity golf tournaments.

For all of his athletic and business accomplishments, Pete Pihos was a complex man. Some of his Indiana teammates disliked his total involvement in the game, bristling at his penchant for practicing just as hard as he played. If you held a tackling dummy and Pihos was bearing down you, you were fair game—especially if you were a freshman. Some blamed his ego. Others said he was simply overzealous. In any case, he had only one real friend on the squad: Dixie Brown said her husband, Howard, "thought the world of Pete."

Though some were put off by his personality, none denied that Pete Pihos played hard and expected others to do the same. In a 1945 postseason talk in Chicago, Bo McMillin said Pihos worked just as hard in practice as in a game. "He didn't spare anything when he would throw a block or make a tackle," Bo told a reporter. "He would come around on Friday afternoon and ask if we couldn't have blocking practice." Mel Groomes, Pihos' backfield mate, called him "a take-charge guy, leading by example. When it came to football, there was none better so far as wanting to win and get the job done." Reserve back Nick Sebek called him "a tough guy. He made you hustle." And Dick Deranek remembered Pete's will to win: "He would see an opponent go down or start limping or something and, since he called the plays, we would go after that guy until they took him out of the game."

"I played one way," Pete recalled fifty years after that championship season: "I played to win."

Perhaps the writers of *Sport* magazine best characterized the guy they called "the old pro" when they wrote: "There's something about Pete Pihos—his face, his muscled body, his sure way on the field—that tells you he has played the game before."

Few have played it better.

-23-
TED KLUSZEWSKI

Argo, Illinois, located in the southern suburbs of Chicago, the home of the Argo Starch factory, and the birthplace of Theodore B. Kluszewski. The Argo Corn Starch Company is now owned by one of the nation's conglomerates. But in the 1930s and 1940s, the Argo factory employed virtually all of the local residents, including many members of the Kluszewski family. When Ted graduated from Argo High School in 1942, he had been a three-sport star: baseball, football (captain) and basketball (captain). It was also there that he met Eleanor Guckel, who would later become his wife. Since his mother and father were deceased, college wasn't an option for Klu, who went to work in the starch factory to help support the family. In his off hours, though, he played a lot of sandlot baseball, and that's how he attracted the attention of Indiana University. One night he attended a McMillin speaking engagement and introduced himself to Bo. That was all that was needed. In 1944 Indiana offered him a scholarship, and he accepted. It was the only way Ted could afford college. So, in the summer of 1944, this twenty-year-old, 6-2, 205-pound behemoth left the starch business and headed to southern Indiana, his plans to wed Eleanor postponed for the time being. He arrived in Bloomington without a suitcase. His wardrobe was on his back. "The underwear and socks he wore had been issued by the athletic department," recalled tackle Bob Joseph. "That's how he started."

One look at Kluszewski and the Indiana coaches knew they had something special. McMillin immediately moved him into the starting lineup for the 1944 season at right end. And as soon as football ended, basketball coach Harry Good had Kluszewski practicing in the Indiana fieldhouse. In the early spring of 1945, Ted was slamming baseballs out of Jordan Field (now the Union Building parking lot). He led the Big Ten in runs batted in and was second in batting.

But three sports took too much time, preventing Klu's periodic visits to Argo to see his family and Eleanor. He dropped basketball, and when football practice resumed in August 1945, Bo was happy to pencil in big Klu at right end. Kluszewski not only defended well for the Hoosiers in 1945, he was a double threat on offense—a receiver and an occasional passer. He scored Indiana's first touchdown against Michigan, threw a completed pass on Indiana's late touchdown drive against Northwestern, and scored the game's only touchdown as Indiana beat Illinois. Against Purdue, he stole back the ball from a Boilermaker to set up Indiana's all-important second touchdown. And late in that title game he took a Raimondi pass for a score.

When the year ended, the experts duly noted Ted's contribution to Indiana's unbeaten season, voting him to the Associated Press and United Press Big Ten first teams. It would be Ted's last hurrah with the Hoosiers. Shortly after the season ended, he was approached by the Cincinnati Reds and signed a professional baseball contract. Not coincidentally, the 1945 Reds team had trained at Indiana that spring because of wartime travel limitations. As a result, they got a good look at Ted during his spring baseball debut. They obviously liked what they had seen. Signing with the Reds wasn't a particularly easy decision for Ted, and he approached teammate Ben Raimondi for advice. "I told him I would beat him up if he didn't," the diminutive Raimondi recalls. "He laughed and signed."

His Indiana teammates recall Klu fondly, often marveling at his skill and power. "He told me that when he went up for a pass, he felt no one could reach higher," said Joe Sowinski. "We would watch him hit those baseballs from old Jordan Field practically to the fieldhouse."

"He was a tremendous athlete," Bob Harbison remembered. "He had probably the biggest arms anybody ever saw—sixteen-inch biceps and nine-inch wrists. And he was a very calm type of person, collected at all times. I never did see him get angry." But George Taliaferro recalls an incident where Ted lost his temper on the practice field. The Hoosiers had a touch scrimmage under way, and freshman halfback Jackie Adams took off around Ted's end. Ted touched him, but Adams ranted and raved that he'd missed. Several plays later, Taliaferro recalled, Adams ran the same play. "Ted damned near killed him—the only time I saw Ted Kluszewski angry." Bob Meyer remembers an incident at the

Michigan game. "Indiana's first punt of the game," Meyer said, "Ted came streaking down the field to make the tackle, and he had really let loose. Fortunately, the Michigan player managed to sidestep; otherwise he would have been down and out. Even the Michigan crowd oooed and ahhhed."

The Kluszewski stories go on. Freshman Tom Schwartz was standing with Ted during practice one day, watching Raimondi throw to the ends. "Raimondi threw as hard as he could, even in practice," Schwartz recalled. "So Kluszewski nudged me and said: 'Watch me—I'll catch his next pass one-handed.' And he did, looking back at Raimondi to see his reaction. And then he did it again and looked back as if to say: 'Is that all the harder you can throw?' "

Despite his many skills, Ted didn't like to practice. (When he got to the Reds, he always abhorred spring training.) And even during games he didn't exactly hustle on every play. Kicker Charlie Armstrong remembers one day when the team was viewing films of the Hoosiers' defense. "The play was in the center of the line, and Ted was at his usual end position. When he saw where the play was going, he took one step forward and stayed there. Bo spoke up and said: 'Well, they're not going to fake old Ted out.' " But when crunch time came, Kluszewski played like the All-American he could have been. Both Pihos and Taliaferro said Klu had unlimited potential. "He didn't know how good he was," Taliaferro said.

On February 9, 1946, Ted and Eleanor married before Kluszewski began his long pro baseball career. He played a partial season with Columbia, South Carolina, leading the Sally League with a .352 average. At the conclusion of the 1947 season—in which Klu hit .377 for Memphis and again led the league, the Reds summoned their slugger to Cincinnati for nine games. And in 1948 he began a big-league career with Cincinnati that lasted until late 1957 when Ted, suffering from a bad back, was traded to the Pittsburgh Pirates for first baseman Dee Fondy. As Eleanor Kluszewski recalled, "The first trade is a shocker because you don't expect it, but after that I think Ted was really pleased." In 1959 he appeared in his only World Series, playing first base for the Chicago White Sox in their losing effort against the Los Angeles Dodgers. He hit three home runs, batted in ten runs and hit .391. Klu hung up his baseball cleats in 1961, after hitting fifteen home runs for the Los Angeles Dodgers.

How good was Ted Kluszewski, the baseball player? Good

enough to have been voted into the Baseball Hall of Fame—if he'd played in New York rather than Cincinnati. His career statistics reflect his ability: 279 home runs, 1,028 runs batted in and a lifetime batting average of .298. Over a four-year period beginning in 1953, Big Ted hit 171 of his home runs. He hit over .300 in each of five straight years beginning in 1952, and in 1954 he led the league in home runs and runs batted in while hitting .326. He was voted to the National League All-Star team from 1953 through 1956. He had Hall of Fame credentials but, because he toiled in relative obscurity in southwest Ohio for most of his career, only a handful of writers voted for his admission to the Hall during the years he was eligible. The Hall does hold at least one piece of the Kluszewski legend, though. Eleanor donated the glove that he wore to set a major league fielding record for first basemen. Even though the Hall of Fame didn't call, Ted has been acclaimed as one of the greatest and most popular Cincinnati players. His popularity continued after he retired; the Jack and Klu Steakhouse in Cincinnati became THE place to dine in the Queen City. In 1969 he joined the Reds as batting coach. During his tenure, Cincinnati became one of the top hitting clubs in baseball, helped in no small part by Ted's tips. He was selected in 1969 as the Reds' first baseman on their greatest team ever.

Could he have been as successful if he had chosen football over baseball? Of course, that question can't be answered accurately. But don't bet that Klu wouldn't have ultimately joined teammate Pete Pihos in the Pro Football Hall of Fame. He was that good. And perhaps his greatest legacy isn't to be found in some museum anyway. Maybe it's better showcased in the tributes from those who knew him best.

He was, by all accounts, a modest man who never promoted himself despite repeated requests from agents. He was compassionate, easy to talk to, a good listener. He was generous—rarely, if ever, charging for his autograph. He was intelligent: "He could pick up a book and grasp everything," recalled IU roommate Bob Miller. And he was kind. "Ted was a gentle giant," said Dixie Brown, "a wonderful, wonderful, person."

Ted Kluszewski died March 29, 1988, at the age of sixty-four—too young for one so deservedly revered in his lifetime.

–24–

HOWARD BROWN

Early in the second quarter of the Purdue game, right halfback Mel Groomes came back to the huddle after a short run and complained that a certain Purdue tackle had been particularly rough on him. Extracurricular roughness wasn't at all uncommon in those days, especially when a white defender tackled a black runner. But guard Howard Brown would have none of it. "We're not going to take that type of treatment of one of our players regardless of his color," Brown announced in the huddle. And so the Hoosiers ran play after play right over the Purdue tackle. "We ran so many plays at that guy—he was just hammered," Mel Groomes recalled. "He straightened up for the rest of the game."

That was Howard Brown, an enthusiastic leader. On the field Brown was one ornery son-of-a-bitch, but after the game he was a friend to everybody. "Howard was an inspirational leader with the team," Bob Harbison recalled. "He just had great leadership. Everybody listened to Howard." Captain Mutt Deal concurred. "Howard was a great one," he said. "So sincere and so much Indiana. He was a great player."

Brown grew up in Dayton, Ohio, one of seven brothers who played football for Dayton's Fairview High School. Though he was a good fullback, he was not highly recruited after graduating in June 1940. Ohio State showed passing interest, but he ended up at Indiana thanks to a recommendation to McMillin from Harry "Tuffy" Brooks, another Dayton product and one of Bo's 1939 freshmen.

Arriving in Bloomington in the late summer of 1940, Brown joined Russ Deal among an outstanding group of freshman prospects. It's likely that he felt comfortable in his choice of schools after watching Billy Hillenbrand and Lou Saban cavort for the freshmen. And although he played only one game as a back in his sophomore year (and was thus given an extra year of eligibility), Brown gained enough experience with the McMillin system to move to right guard in 1942. At 5-11, 205 pounds, Brown started in the front line with Deal, Pihos and fellow juniors Fred Huff, Eddie Bell and Ted Hasapes. Howard even had his head shaved as a symbol of team unity, Pihos recalled, thus earning the nickname "Goon" Brown.

After an outstanding 1942 season, it's little wonder McMillin labeled his 1943 returnees his "Dream Team." Unfortunately, after 1943 spring practice, the Dream Team became a casualty of the war. By mid-year, Howard Brown was in the infantry. Allied bombers had been raining destruction on Germany and Italy that summer in what some viewed as a prelude to invasion. However, a year passed before the Allies invaded "Fortress Europe." After D-Day, June 6, 1944, it became a soldier's war, particularly for the infantry. Before the fighting ended in Europe the following May, Sgt. Howard Brown had been wounded three times. His valor had earned him a Purple Heart and two Oak-leaf Clusters.

Fast-forward to Dayton, Ohio, Friday evening, September 21, 1945: Michigan and the Hoosiers were to meet in Ann Arbor the next day. Brown, still in the service, was home in Dayton that evening when Bo called. "Bo said that he had already been in touch with Pihos, who had also just returned from Europe, and he wanted us to meet him Monday in Indianapolis," Brown said later. "We had a forty-five-day furlough before our discharge papers came through, and said we might as well enroll and play football." When Pihos and Brown got to the Athletic Club in downtown Indianapolis that Monday, they found McMillin ready to address the Downtown Quarterback Club. He introduced the two returnees, but avoided questions about the timing of their return. However, the next day, Pihos and Brown reported to practice. By week's end these two decorated war heroes were in Evanston, Illinois, warming up for Indiana's game with Northwestern. Pihos recalled that he and Brown roomed together that Friday night at the Edgewater Beach Hotel. "If Bo had seen us that night before the game, he would have kicked us off of the team," Pihos remembered with a chuckle. "We had just gotten back from fighting a damn war, and we had just a little too much to drink." It didn't affect their play the next day, though. Pihos played fifty-three minutes in that game; Brown, fifty-two. And Brown said at the time that Pihos had been knocked unconscious, recovering in time to catch the pass that enabled Indiana to tie the score.

For the rest of the 1945 season, Howard Brown did everything humanly possible to assure an undefeated season for his beloved Indiana—not just with his outstanding play at right guard, but also in his relationships with the players and coaches. When Mel Groomes needed a boost, Brown put his arm around his shoulder and said, "Don't worry." Howard Wright, a little-used reserve, remembered Brown as a class act. "I was lowest man on the totem pole, but he was so nice to me," Wright recalled. "A wonderful, wonderful person." Joe Sowinski said: "Howard Brown was well-liked and respected by the ballplayers. He was a guy who went through quite a bit when he was in Europe. A very compassionate person, he always made sure the boys went to church." At a time when black players were rarely recruited by major schools, the Hoosiers had six on their 1945 roster. This often made road trips difficult, so McMillin asked Howard if he would room with one of the black players to break the ice. "Of course he did," Bob Joseph recalled. "Howard was the perfect person for the job."

At the end of the 1945 season, Brown was named an American Football Coaches Association second-team All-American. He also was rewarded by his teammates, who voted him their captain for 1946. In addition, he was named this championship team's most valuable player, a tribute to his preeminent role during a special season. Brown played two more years at Indiana, helping the Hoosiers compile two more winning records. He never played for a losing team at IU after 1941. In December 1946, he wed his Sigma Kappa sweetheart at Indiana, Dixie Pepple. He was team captain again his senior year, again earning most-valuable-player status at season's end.

Postseason honors included a spot on the East team for the traditional East-West Shrine Game on New Year's Day 1948. Brown started at guard, helping power the East to a 40–6 win in San Francisco. And in August 1948, just before his first pro season, he was on the roster for the *Chicago Tribune* All-Star Game.

Brown was drafted by Green Bay, but never played a down for the Packers. Bo McMillin, who had assumed the head coaching job at Detroit in 1948, immediately traded two regulars to get his boy to Detroit. The three years with the Lions were dreadful for McMillin. Though he tried mightily to improve Detroit's fortunes, the Lions were only 12–24 during that span. After a mediocre 1950 season, Bo's contract was bought and Brown left.

With his playing career over, Brown returned to Blooming-ton in 1951 as line coach for the Hoosiers under head coach Clyde Smith. And when Smith resigned during the 1952 season, Brown went with him to Arizona, where he built a solid line for the Sun Devils. In 1954, Hoosier coach Bernie Crimmins called Brown back to his alma mater as freshman football coach. Brown, then thirty-two, never left Indiana until his death twenty-one years later. In those years, Howard Brown made many friends, espe-cially among the freshman athletes he helped mold. "I've always had a desire to help kids," he said at the time. "I really like kids and I've devoted my life to coaching them." Howard continued to participate in alumni affairs at Indiana University. And in 1969, along with Pihos and Taliaferro, he was named to the all-time Hoosier squad, garnering more votes then any other interior line-man.

By 1966, the forty-four-year-old Brown and wife Dixie had three sons, Bob, Ted, and Bill. The oldest, Bob, opted to attend the U.S. Military Academy that fall after considering Purdue (much to his dad's dismay). In 1970, Lieutenant Bob Brown gradu-ated from West Point in the top five percent of his class. He was deployed to Vietnam on September 7, 1971, and on October 15, he was wounded at Da Nang. Bob Brown died two days later. He was only twenty-three years old.

Dixie Brown said her husband never recovered from their son's death. She recalls that, before Bob left for Vietnam, he wrote his dad a marvelous letter, indicating that he'd been accepted at Harvard's MBA program after his tour of duty. "I'm telling you," Dixie said, "losing a spouse is terrible, but losing a child when they are so young, it's the worst thing in the world." After his son's death, Brown's health became a concern. He suffered a heart attack in 1973 and, on doctor's orders, he lost forty-five pounds and became a dedicated jogger. Two years later, in the early morn-ing of April 4, 1975, he returned to his Bloomington home after a jog. At approximately 6:30 A.M., the man they called Mr. Indiana was dead.

Brown's funeral on Monday, April 7, drew a large crowd to the First Central Methodist Church in Bloomington. To say Howard Brown was well-liked doesn't do justice to the man. Af-ter his death, the Indiana University Varsity Club established a

Howard Brown Endowment Fund for student athletes. And as a fitting tribute to their leader, his friends and teammates contributed half a million dollars within a year.

Asked what her husband might consider his legacy, Dixie Brown said, thinking not of his on-field exploits, but of his effect on the boys he later coached: "I think he would like to be remembered as having contributed to these young men and their lives and what they did later on. And for his loyalty and the fact that he loved Indiana University so much." Brown's 1945 teammates have their own fond memories. Veteran back Dick Deranek called him "a tremendous leader and player." To guard Frank Ciolli, whom Brown replaced in 1945, he was "a leader and a gentlemen." But George Taliaferro said it best: "God only made one Howard Brown—I mean off the field and on the field. He was the quintessential human being."

Perhaps one final story best illustrates Brown's character. On February 4, 1950, while living in Detroit, he was driving down a street when a man ran out of a gasoline station, yelling: "I've been robbed!" Brown immediately leaped from his car and tackled one of the fleeing suspects. When police arrived, Brown was holding his dazed victim "with all the power that gained him All-America recognition at Indiana University in 1947," reported the *Detroit Times*.

Praised for his heroism, Brown demurred good-naturedly. "Anyone could have done what I did," he said. "I just threw him down and held him for the police. He wasn't a very good broken-field runner." When asked if it was a flying tackle that had subdued the robber, Brown laughed and quipped: "I don't think it was a flying tackle. That's illegal and would have meant a fifteen-yard penalty."

Now, wasn't that just like Howard Brown?

–25–
JOHN GOLDSBERRY

At 6 feet tall and 235 pounds, John Goldsberry wasn't the biggest lineman ever to play at Indiana. But when he suited up for the Hoosiers in 1945, he was the fastest. He had prepped at John Adams High School in South Bend, where he was named the school's outstanding athlete his senior year, a year that marked his second consecutive state shotput championship. Of course he also played football, earning Northern Indiana all-conference consideration in 1944.

Goldsberry's athletic ability came naturally. His father, Alonzo Goldsberry, had starred at Wabash College in football, basketball and baseball. One of the greatest athletes ever to attend the Crawfordsville school, Alonzo coached his son at John Adams from 1943 to 1945. McMillin personally recruited young Goldsberry, and no one could outcharm Bo. According to John's widow, Barbara, the Colonel put an arm around John's anxious mother and said: "Now, don't you worry. We'll take care of him." So, in late June 1945, with his mother put at ease, Goldsberry joined his freshman teammates for summer football drills in sultry Bloomington. By mid-September, he had impressed Bo and his staff so highly that he was one of three freshmen in the starting lineup against Michigan on September 22. Opening at right tackle and ultimately playing between Brown and Kluszewski, Goldsberry was an integral part of the front line that paved the way to Indiana's success.

In the years that followed 1945, Goldsberry continued to contribute, though the Hoosiers' fortunes faded. McMillin left in 1947, and John played his last year, 1948, for Hoosier coach Clyde Smith, having been elected captain by his teammates. But a knee injury suffered against Iowa the previous year had robbed him of some of his quickness. Even so, he made All Big Ten honorable mention his last three years at Indiana and played in the *Chicago Tribune* All-Star Game in August 1949.

Following his graduation from the IU School of Business, Goldsberry was drafted by the Chicago Cardinals, and for the next two years he helped Chicago to a winning record. Among his teammates were Elmer Angsman of Notre Dame, Charlie Trippi of Georgia, Pat Harder of Wisconsin and former Indiana teammate Bob Ravensberg. In February 1951, when McMillin left the Detroit Lions for the Philadelphia Eagles, one of Bo's first calls was to his former right tackle. But the lingering effects of the knee injury convinced Big John that the risk of further damage wasn't worth the money. Though surgery had repaired his knee, Goldsberry had lost the speed that had set him apart from other linemen, and his short stint with the Cardinals had been wracked with pain. His wife, the former Barbara Sykes, whom Goldsberry had met during the IU summer session of 1947, remembers letters she received from her sweetheart which mentioned the long hours he'd spent in the Cardinals' whirlpool. And shortly after Bo's call, Goldsberry chose family life over football. He and Barbara were married on March 11, 1951.

After his football career, Goldsberry sold insurance in his hometown of South Bend. Success in insurance sales came easily for John with his calm demeanor, sense of humor and natural interest in people. Barbara recalled his ability to communicate, especially with the older ladies. "He was really a kind, gentle person—which the older women appreciated."

John and Barbara raised three children, two sons and a daughter. "He was very good with the children," Barbara remembered. "A good disciplinarian, but he never used abusive language." He enjoyed his leisure time—especially fishing and his weekly poker game with his buddies—and he was a generous person. "When he was with the Cardinals, he would send his check home—unopened—to his mother," Barbara recalled. "One Christmas, a teammate with a family at home ran out of money. My husband gave him money, and then he played poker and lived on what was left."

John Goldsberry's love of food was legendary. "He did love to eat, and he was heavy," Barbara admitted, and some of his 1945 teammates recalled his large appetite. "Every time we would take a trip, he would find the best hamburger place and have a meal before the team ate," George Taliaferro recalled. Dixie and Howard Brown often had John over for dinner, and Dixie remembered: "All you had to do was put a bowl of mashed potatoes and gravy on the table, and he was off and running." Nick Sebek said: "I never saw a guy eat so many damn hot dogs and hamburgers in my life!"

In the fall of 1970, Indiana University reunited its heroes of 1945 for their twenty-fifth reunion, a get-together that brought back all of these memories, and a wealth of others. Barbara remembered John giving Mel Groomes a big hug. "They were all just really thrilled." Two years later, just a few months before his and Barbara's twenty-first wedding anniversary, John Goldsberry died suddenly on January 24, 1972. He was only forty-five years old. Besides Barbara, he left their three children, the youngest only seventeen.

Like all of the Indiana players in 1945, John Goldsberry had a role to play, and he played it well. Quick, strong and quite mature for an eighteen-year-old, the big freshman was an important part of the line that has seen few equals in the history of Indiana football. "For his size, I don't think I've ever seen a lineman as fast and tough as John," said Frank Ciolli. "John was one of the first real big players that I had ever seen," fellow lineman Bob Harbison said. "He was very mobile for his size . . . and he had a great attitude." It was that attitude, and his wonderful sense of humor, that Ben Raimondi remembered most about John Goldsberry. Bullet Ben said he'll never forget how the big guy "always put a smile on your face."

What better way to be remembered?

—THE COACH—

–26–
Bo McMillin

Alvin Nugent McMillin was one of twelve children born to a hard-working family in Prairie Hill, Texas, a small town seventeen miles from Waco. The year was 1895—a rough-and-tumble time in the Southwest. Rural life was hard. Sanitation was primitive, electricity and paved roads were years away. What later became the state of Oklahoma was still Indian territory. And coincidently, the first professional football game was played that year in Latrobe, Pennsylvania.

Several years later, young McMillin accompanied his family to Fort Worth, where Alvin became known as Bo, probably a nick-name given him by one of his cousins. With Bo's dad working in Fort Worth and the family settled in for a long stay, McMillin began to develop an interest in sports while attending Fort Worth North High School. Bo's father died in 1911, but by 1912, under the tutelage of North football coach Robert "Chief" Meyers, Bo became a member of the football, basketball, and baseball teams. After four years of success, particularly in football, Bo followed Meyers to Centre College in Danville, Kentucky, where the Chief, an alumnus of the school, had been named head football coach. Not surprisingly, several of McMillin's teammates at North also enrolled at Centre, significantly swelling the school's enrollment of fewer than four hundred students.

Shortly after arriving at Centre, Meyers appointed himself athletic director and astutely hired baseball umpire Charlie Moran as the school's football coach. Moran, McMillin and Meyers made a great triumvirate. With McMillin at quarterback, Centre began to win. Bo took time off in 1918 to serve his country, but he returned the following year, declining an offer to play pro-fessional baseball for five years at the then princely sum of ten thousand dollars per year. The Praying Colonels, as Centre's players became known because of their pregame prayers, went undefeated in 1919, and McMillin was named an All-American.

During this era, Eastern schools dominated college football, particularly the Harvard Crimson. Harvard was in the middle of a long winning streak when it consented to play tiny Centre in 1920. True to form, the Crimson won handily, 31–14. But a year later, on October 21, 1921, with the Harvard win streak at twenty-five, Centre got its revenge. Led by McMillin, the Colonels toppled mighty Harvard 6–0. It was a stunning upset, and it propelled young McMillin into national prominence.

When the 1921 season ended, officials at Centenary College, aware of Bo's exploits, offered him the head coaching job at the Shreveport, Louisiana, school. Although he lacked enough credits to graduate from Centre, Bo took the reins at Centenary and over the next three years won twenty-five of twenty-eight games, most by large margins. Married in 1922, Bo became a father in 1923 when little Fleurette McMillin arrived. They nicknamed her "BoPeep."

Flushed with success in the South, McMillin accepted a position with Geneva College in Pennsylvania in 1925, taking three Centenary regulars with him. Again he was a winner, and in his first year he again beat Harvard. But tragedy struck the family in 1926. Bo's wife died of pneumonia, and BoPeep, herself nearly a victim of the disease, went to live with family members. Bo, having led Geneva to an unbeaten season in 1927 and a record of twenty-seven victories in thirty-three games, accepted the head coaching job at a larger school, Kansas State College. Six years at that school produced another winning record for McMillin. It also produced a new family. Bo married a Kansas State coed in 1928, a marriage that ultimately produced two sons and two daughters. In 1934, Bo departed Kansas State, leaving behind a team that gave new head coach Lynn "Pappy" Waldorf the school's first Big Six Championship.

While Pappy rejoiced in Manhattan, Kansas, Bo rebuilt in Bloomington, Indiana. When it came to football, Indiana University had long been a Big Ten doormat. The last coach with a winning record had left in 1921. In the thirteen years that followed, the Hoosiers were 33–54 and went through four coaches. McMillin knew he faced a stiff challenge as coach of the downtrodden Hoosiers. It turned out to be one of the best investments either party ever made.

In the big-time arena for the first time, McMillin faced a formidable recruiting task at Indiana in 1934. High school kids in the Hoosier state played basketball, not football, and talent was thin within the state. And in the twenties, instead of building a large stadium comparable to those at Michigan, Illinois and Ohio State, Indiana chose to build a small, horseshoe-shaped facility seating only about twenty-two thousand. University officials probably had no choice because they had little money. Indiana's Memorial Stadium was attractive, but it was far too small to create big pay days on autumn Saturdays.

Arriving by train in 1934, the dapper McMillin might have felt a bit apprehensive when neither athletic director Zora Clevenger nor interim head coach Billy Hayes was on hand to greet him (both were out of town). But a banquet held that spring to introduce Bo drew fifteen-hundred people. And the silver-haired orator from Prairie Hill didn't disappoint. His first two proclamations set the tone for the next fourteen years: "I'm not going to be the sexton of any cemetery at Indiana University," he announced, adding: "I've seen sicker cats get well." The crowd was on its feet, cheering. Indiana finally had its coach.

The first four seasons under McMillin were like a cool breeze on a hot summer day. All at once, the Hoosiers became competitive. Bo and his "po' little boys" avoided a losing season each year and beat rival Purdue three times. In addition, Indiana pulled off 1937's football upset by beating powerful Ohio State 10–0. In those four years, Indiana played only twelve games in Bloomington.

McMillin entered his fifth year with optimism, but his punchless Hoosiers lost six games in 1938, scoring only three touchdowns the entire season. Only two wins were chalked up in 1939, and the 1940 and 1941 seasons were likewise losers. Some alumni began to grumble that perhaps the Colonel should be demoted, but McMillin hadn't changed between 1938 and 1941. It was a matter of personnel, along with an increase in the level of competition. Besides, Bo was just getting started.

In the fall of 1940, his comeback began with Bo's best freshman class ever, a group that included the kid everybody wanted that fall, Billy Hillenbrand of Evansville, along with talented Lou Saban of Chicago. A year later, he brought together another fine group of freshmen, including a hard-nosed end from Chicago named Pete Pihos.

The attack on Pearl Harbor in December 1941 dramatically changed the country's priorities. Bo did manage to maintain most of his squad the next year, a season that produced seven wins and the promise of more victories in the years ahead. But by 1943, with most of Indiana's opponents stocked with service trainees straight from football squads on other campuses, McMillin could only hope for miracles. In the fall of 1943, thirty-nine young men showed up on campus for Bo's tenth year; thirty-four were freshmen. And yet the Hoosiers held their own, staying competitive in all but the Michigan and Great Lakes games while compiling a 4–4–2 record. Indiana football became even more entertaining in 1944. The Hoosiers won seven of ten games that year, though few fans had enough gas stamps to venture to Bloomington on any given Saturday.

Of course, McMillin's football career hit its zenith with the Hoosiers' championship season. After being named Man of the Year and Coach of the Year for 1945, he became the unofficial banquet speaker of the year for 1946. However, his many absences from campus and the 1946 military draft combined to complicate Bo's early-season routine in 1946. This helped prevent Indiana from being the first Big Ten team to play in the Rose Bowl under the 1946 arrangement between the Big Ten and the Pacific Coast Conference. After coaching the College All-Stars to a 16–0 win over the Los Angeles Rams in August 1946, Bo was late getting back to campus that fall and then was greeted by a large squad of 1945 holdovers and veterans from other seasons. It took him a while to get organized; in the meantime, the Hoosiers were upset by Cincinnati in their opener and failed to score the next week, falling 21–0 to Michigan. A midseason loss to Iowa put the Hoosiers out of the running for the Roses. Still, Illinois, the eventual Rose Bowl winner, fell 14–7 to the Hoosiers that year at Bloomington.

By 1947, not even Bo's charm and coaching ability could do the trick. Indiana won only five games. The small stadium, Bloomington's comparatively remote location, and the lack of sufficient depth to play two-platoon football all chipped away at Indiana's fortunes. In 1946, in order to boost McMillin's income, the university had appointed him athletic director as well as coach, but in the end it wasn't enough. Impressed by Bo's performance as the winning coach in the '46 College All-Star game, the Detroit Lions made Bo an offer he finally couldn't refuse following the 1947 season. IU Chancellor Herman B Wells, then president of the university, recalled a conversation with McMillin prior to Bo's departure. "I told him: 'You won't be as happy there as you'd be here.' Bo said: 'I know it.' I told him: 'I'll do everything I can to keep you here.' McMillin replied: 'I've got a young family and I need to make more money—more than you can pay me. I don't want to do it, but I have to.' " Bo was right; he shouldn't have left. His three-year stint in Detroit was fraught with frustration and dissension, and the team's 12–24 record during that period fueled impatience in the Lions' front office. Detroit bought out Bo's contract after the 1950 season. Not surprisingly, the team he had assembled between 1948 and 1951 went on to become a championship squad in the early 1950s.

If Detroit didn't want McMillin, then the Philadelphia Eagles did, and they hired him for the 1951 season. It would be his last. The Eagles went 6–6 that year, with Bo no doubt suffering silently from the cancer that eventually killed him. Shortly after the season ended, he asked to return to his beloved Bloomington. At 2:30 A.M. on March 31, 1952, Bo McMillin died at age fifty-seven.

Friends and admirers from across the country attended the funeral. Notre Dame sent coach Frank Leahy and "Moose" Krause. Floral tributes came from dozens of schools and organizations, including the Harvard Athletic Association. There was no eulogy. Herman B Wells had said it all five days after Indiana had won its championship in 1945:

> "Our coach is unexcelled as a master teacher of football—but that is not all. He is the devoted servant of this institution, its extraordinary ambassador of goodwill, an inspiration to changing generations of Indiana men and women, a Christian gentleman and a leader of men."

Those who knew Bo McMillin never forgot his integrity, style and coaching skill. "A great coach—a gentlemen. They didn't come any better," said Chicago-born tailback Bob Miller. "The players respected him, and he was interested in their well being." Of course, being interested sometimes meant being tough, and Bo knew the importance of discipline. "There was no profanity on the field, and he didn't take any guff from his players," recalled tackle Mutt Deal. Not even All-American Pete Pihos was exempt (although one player recalled an instance where Bo sent in a substitute for Pete—and Pete promptly sent him back. Pihos wasn't ready to come out yet, so the substitute stayed on the bench).

In the ever-changing world of college football, only innovative coaches are consistent winners, and few could match McMillin's knack for innovation. At Kansas State he introduced a five-man backfield. At Indiana he took Clark Shaughnessy's T-formation and created his own "cockeyed-T," with one back split out. On defense, he pulled his ends off the line of scrimmage to form the first 4–4 defense. Although other coaches later claimed credit, it was McMillin who pioneered the 4–4 in 1945. "Bo's plays are still being used by pro teams," Ben Raimondi said more than forty years after his coach's death. "Bo was one of the smartest of them all."

He was also intensely competitive—a spirit he transferred to his players. "Bo put the idea into our heads that we could win," said lineman Bob Harbison. "I think a lot of that carried over into our lives. That's what he gave us: We were winners and we could win." He also taught them the importance of meticulous preparation. No detail escaped him. Kicker Charlie Armstrong recalls Bo holding a stopwatch while Armstrong kicked extra points. "He wanted the ball kicked between one and one-tenth and one and two-tenths of a second from the time it was snapped," Armstrong said.

But it was Bo McMillin the man, not the coach, who left the deepest impression on his players. "He was loyal to you and would do anything for you," said halfback Dick Deranek. "His door was always open; we could go in anytime we wanted, and he took care of us." He was a father figure to all of his players—particularly to Pihos, Cannady and Kluszewski, all of whom had lost their fathers before coming to Indiana. "Bo McMillin was just like a daddy to me," John Cannady said. "He was a great man."

"Bo was very kind to me," recalled Nick Sebek, a freshman in 1945. "I was only one of two kids from North Tonawanda, New York, that he kept after that summer. I cried when he told me I was going to stay. I was just a seventeen-year-old kid getting beat up by the varsity. He treated me like a son. At the Catholic church on Sundays, you always stuck your head up to make sure Bo saw you."

What more can be said about McMillin—dedicated family

man, teacher, this color-blind and imaginative coach and mes-
merizing speaker? Two of his greatest stars remember him fondly.
"He was a good person—honest, sincere and a family man," Pete
Pihos recalled. "We all loved him." And George Taliaferro: "Bo
was just an incredible human being."

In 1982 McMillin was inducted into the Indiana University
Intercollegiate Athletic Hall of Fame. Three decades earlier, in
1951, he'd been awarded a similar honor by the College Football
Hall of Fame—but as a player, not a coach. Bo McMillin won 144
of the 224 games he coached over a twenty-six-year career—a
winning percentage of more than 64 percent. He did more than
win, though. As player after player will attest, he made men out
of boys, taught them fair play and gave them a firm foundation
for their lives after football. McMillin said, "My life belongs to
football, family and God."

As Winston Churchill once pointed out: "One mark of a great
man is the power of making lasting impressions upon the people
he meets."

Bo McMillin did just that.

(Left) Alvin Nugent "Bo" McMillin made his athletic mark early, starring as a Texas high-schooler, then going on to tiny Centre College in Danville, Kentucky.

(Below) It was as Centre's quarterback that Bo came to national prominence, leading the Praying Colonels to a stunning upset over mighty Harvard in 1921, ending the Crimson's 25-game winning streak.

McMillin, who came to Indiana from Kansas State in 1934 and stayed at the Hoosiers' helm through the 1947 season, never lost his eye for detail, especially on the practice field.

(Below) McMillin (center) with assistants (from left): Charles McDaniel, John Kovatch, Paul "Pooch" Harrell, and Gordon R. Fisher. (missing: "Timmy" Temerario, "Swede" Anderson).

The Big Ten, 1967
After the Hoosiers' Big Ten championship, McMillin was named
national coach of the year. That honor, coupled with his natural
gift of gab, led to a successful stint on the banquet circuit.

This photograph, taken by an Associated Press photographer in 1946, shows Bo with his sons Mike (left) and Nugent on the IU practice field. It seems to capture what many players felt about McMillin and what star Pete Pihos said best: "He was a good person—honest, sincere, and a family man. We all loved him." Bo left IU after this photo was taken and died of cancer five years later.

—Epilogue—

December 1945 was the last month in a year that may ultimately be judged the most significant and tumultuous in the twentieth century. In those 365 days, the old order died and a new one was born.

That month, in the afterglow of war's end and still flush from the school's first football championship, the Indiana campus continued in its euphoria. The first peacetime holiday season since 1940! On December 6, the YWCA Christmas party kicked off the Christmas-on-campus celebration, followed by the opening of formal season. The next day, Jimmy Jay and his orchestra played for dancers at Alumni Hall. A week later, on December 15, snow and five-degree temperatures did nothing to discourage attendance at the Dames Ball.

Nor had the team been forgotten. Lettermen had been named—including, as McMillin had promised, Bob Meyer, the sophomore center who had broken his leg at Ann Arbor and played but twenty minutes in 1945. On December 11, the Bloomington Chamber of Commerce honored Bo and his boys the same day the sportswriters voted Indiana's football season as the number-two surprise of the season. (Great Lakes' 35–7 drubbing of Notre Dame was number one.) The Hoosiers trekked to Indianapolis on December 18 to be honored by The Indiana University Club.

Since basketball season was under way, members of the football team formed a squad called Nick's Picks to compete against the varsity "B" team—all for charity. Ciolli, Taliaferro, the Raven, Deranek, Groomes and Big Klu all played.

Finally, the last day of classes arrived—Friday, December 21. At 11 A.M., by bus, train, car or thumb, the students headed home harboring a well-founded hope for a yuletide season of peace and good will.

When they returned in January, they expected a different Indiana campus as the school began its transition to postwar prosperity. Expanded faculty and curriculum, larger buildings, living space for the fourteen hundred war veterans expected to enroll in February, the Woodlawn Trailer Courts—all were on the agenda to meet the enrollment of ten thousand expected for the following year.

New Year's Day 1946 marked a new beginning, in Bloomington and all over the world. It was a year of great promise earned at great price—a price that all agreed must never be paid again. That afternoon, as in years past, the few students on campus before the January 4 resumption of classes gathered at the Union or in their rooms to hear the broadcast of the Rose Bowl game. This year Alabama faced the University of Southern California; the automatic inclusion of the Big Ten winner would become a reality in '46. Perhaps the '45 champs could repeat. . . .

No matter what the future held for Indiana football, though, the 1945 team had given birth to a legacy with its win on November 24. The Hoosiers of 1946 and subsequent years would have their share of wins, perhaps even earn another championship. But to the students, alumni and other fans who rallied to Indiana's cause that Hoosier autumn, this was one moment that couldn't be replicated. It would last forever.

The twin towers at the east end of what was once old Memorial Stadium still stand as a monument to the Hoosier's moment in the sun. This photo, taken fifty years to the hour after IU's historic win over Purdue on November 24, 1945, has the same late-afternoon glow that Indiana players and fans basked in half a century ago.

Courtesy I. Will Counts, Bloomington

Nick Judy, IU Support Services

In 1995, several of the surviving members of the '45 team gathered for the golden anniversary of the championship. (From left): Bob Harbison, Bob Meyer, Charlie Armstrong, Tom Schwartz, Russ Deal, Bob Miller (kneeling), Joe Sowinski, Mel Groomes (seated), Larry Napolitan, George Taliaferro, Frank Ciolli, Bill Bradley, and Dick Deranek.